This Book Is

Protected by
Instant IP

"Kris has been guiding business owners for years—his no-nonsense approach is exactly what owners need. This book is a clear and direct instructional manual on how to fine-tune your meetings and turn them into a productivity machine. All entrepreneurs should follow this program and implement meetings that don't suck.

— **Dr. Craig West,** Founder and Chairman of Succession Plus

MEETINGS
KINDA SUCK

MEETINGS KINDA SUCK

Kris Snyder

Professional EOS Implementer®

Published by Igniting Souls
PO Box 43, Powell, OH 43065
IgnitingSouls.com

LCCN: 2026907079
Paperback ISBN: 978-1-63680-640-2
Hardback ISBN: 978-1-63680-641-9
eBook ISBN: 978-1-63680-642-6

Available in paperback, hardcover, e-book, and audiobook.

Any Internet addresses (websites, blogs, etc.) and telephone numbers printed in this book are offered as a resource. They are not intended in any way to be or imply an endorsement by Igniting Souls, nor does Igniting Souls vouch for the content of these sites and numbers for the life of this book.

Some names and identifying details may have been changed to protect the privacy of individuals.

EOS®, The Entrepreneurial Operating System®, Traction®, and EOS Implementer® are registered trademarks owned by EOS Worldwide, LLC. For a complete list of trademarks owned by EOS Worldwide throughout this book, please visit branding.eosworldwide.com/eos-trademarks/.

The content of this book reflects the author's personal experiences, opinions, and interpretations. The inclusion of any individual, living or deceased, or any organization or entity, is not intended to malign, defame, or harm the reputation of such persons or entities. All statements regarding individuals are solely the author's perspective and do not represent verified facts unless expressly cited to a verifiable source.

The publisher has not independently investigated or confirmed the accuracy of any such references and disclaims all responsibility for them. Nothing in this book should be construed as factual assertions about the character, conduct, or reputation of any individual or entity mentioned. Any resemblance to persons living or dead is purely coincidental unless explicitly stated.

The publisher expressly disclaims liability for any alleged loss, damage, or injury arising from any perceived defamatory content or reliance upon statements within this work. Responsibility for the views, depictions, and representations rests solely with the author.

The superscript symbol IP listed throughout this book is known as the unique certification mark created and owned by Instant IP®. Its use signifies that the corresponding expression (words, phrases, chart, graph, etc.) has been protected by Instant IP® via smart contract. Instant IP® is designed with the patented smart contract solution (US Patent: 11,928,748), which creates an immutable time-stamped first layer and fast layer identifying the moment in time an idea is filed on the blockchain. This solution can be used in defending intellectual property protection. Infringing upon the respective intellectual property, i.e., IP, is subject to and punishable in a court of law.

DEDICATION

*For anyone who's ever looked at their calendar and thought,
"When do I do my real job?" May your meetings be fewer, sharper,
and the kind you look forward to. And may you reclaim enough
time to remember why you loved this work in the first place.*

TABLE OF CONTENTS

FOREWORD

I've spent nearly thirty years in rooms where the real work of a business either happens or doesn't.

Not the corner office. Not the strategy retreat. The meeting room. The weekly meeting pulse. The moment a leadership team sits down together and either moves the business forward or wastes another hour pretending to.

As the Integrator of EOS Worldwide, meetings are my operating environment. They're where I translate vision into execution, where I hold the team accountable to our Rocks, where we IDS the issues standing between us and what matters most. The Level 10 Meeting isn't a box I check. It's the single most important ninety minutes of my week. Every week. Because when that works, everything downstream works: the clarity, the follow-through, the results, the team health, the culture.

And when it doesn't? You feel it everywhere.

The energy drains. Decisions stall. Trust erodes quietly. Your best people start wondering if anyone's actually steering the ship. I've lived that reality, and I've watched hundreds of leadership teams live it too. Meetings are where EOS initially lives or dies in a company. Full stop.

That's why this book matters.

Kris Snyder has written something I wish existed when I was earlier in my career, an honest, practical, session-room-tested guide to fixing the thing most leaders complain about but few have the discipline to change. *Meetings Kinda Suck* isn't theory from the sidelines. It's from someone who has successfully built companies, coached leadership teams through real problems, and done the hard work of sitting in the room when things get uncomfortable. Kris enters the danger. You'll feel that on every page.

What I appreciate most about this book is that Kris understands something many people miss: meetings move human energy. They're not simply about agendas and action items. They're about whether the people in the room feel safe enough to speak up, focused enough to solve real issues, and clear enough to leave and execute. When meetings are done well, they manage human energy for the greater good. They create the conditions where a team can do its best thinking together and then go make it real.

This is the Integrator's world. I live in the space between the Visionary's ideas and the team's capacity to make them real. I own the operating system and the meeting pulse. I protect the structure that makes great meetings possible. And while I don't always facilitate every meeting myself, I make sure the right person does. In EOS, facilitation belongs to whoever is best qualified to keep the room honest, focused, and moving forward. Sometimes that's me. Often it's another leader on the team who brings the right combination of courage and discipline to hold the space. The Integrator's job is to ensure the system works, that IDS actually solves root issues and makes them go away forever, that the quiet voice gets pulled in, and that after the meeting ends, we're 100 percent aligned and on the same page. Week after week, we're making steady, consistent progress. One step at a time.

Kris gets this. He writes about facilitation, role clarity, the Visionary's impact on room dynamics, the psychology of why people don't speak up, all of it grounded in real stories and real consequences. He connects the dots between meeting discipline and culture in a way that is both practical and deeply people-centric.

Because here's what I know to be true after running on EOS every single day: when your meetings work, your people feel valued. They feel heard. They have clarity of direction and confidence in execution toward real, simple results. They stop dreading Mondays and start looking forward to them. And that shift (from meetings as a time sink to meetings as the heartbeat of the business) is what allows entrepreneurs and their teams to get everything they want from their businesses. It supports culture. It strengthens team health. It changes how people experience their work and their lives.

That's not a small thing. That's everything.

Kris wrote this book for the leaders who know their meetings need to be better and are willing to do the work to get there. He wrote it with the kind of honesty and humor that makes you laugh while you're also thinking, "Oh wow, we've done that!" And he wrote it with enough practical tools that you can start fixing things this week. Not next quarter. This week.

Read this book. Take it seriously. Run your next meeting with more intention. Rate it. Adjust. Do it again. Show up and lead well. Put the love into making every meeting, every interaction, count. Consistently.

Your team deserves it. Your business depends on it.

And trust me, when you get this right, everything changes.

With encouragement and focus,
Kelly Knight
Integrator/President, EOS Worldwide
Author, *People – Dare to Build an Intentional Culture*

INTRODUCTION

Here's the thing about meetings: they're either the heartbeat of your business or the thing slowly killing the business.

And most of the time? They're slowly killing the business.

I've spent twenty-two years building companies, coaching leadership teams, and sitting through more meetings than any 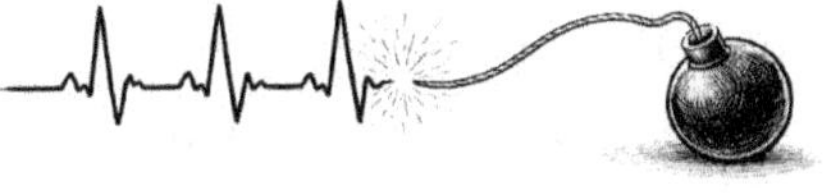 human should endure. I've been in meetings so bad they made me question my career choices. I've run meetings that bombed. I've fixed meetings that turned entire companies around. And here's what I've learned: meetings don't suck because meetings are inherently terrible. They suck because nobody taught us how to run them.

Think about this. You go to school for years. You learn calculus, history, and how to write a five-paragraph essay. But running a productive meeting? Making decisions as a team? Solving real problems in real time while keeping everyone engaged and moving forward? Nope. We're supposed to figure this out on our own, or worse, we learn on the job from others who were never taught, and the chain continues.

So we wing the thing. We continue to copy what we've seen other people do. We throw "Weekly Sync" on the calendar and hope for the best. And then we wonder why everyone's checking email, why nothing gets decided, why the same issues keep coming up week after week.

Meetings Kinda Suck is the first book in a series. The next one, *Work Shouldn't Suck,* is about the broader experience of work, including the culture, the people, and the moments making you want to stay or run for the exit. But here, we're focusing on the single biggest time drain, energy killer, and culture destroyer in most organizations: bad meetings.

When your meetings suck, your business feels it. People get frustrated, and your best talent starts to check out. Decisions take longer, problems stick around, and meetings become something you have to get through instead of something to help you do your job.

When meetings work, everything feels different. Decisions happen faster, they are made with supporting data, and people leave focused and ready to move forward.

This book is about fixing meetings so they work. So they don't suck. So your team values them and treats them like the heartbeat of the business, not a time sink.

If you've ever sat in a meeting and thought, "Why am I here?" this book is for you.

For Visionaries[1], tired of rehashing the same problems. For Integrators[2] quietly carrying too much. For team leads who want to run meetings working. For anyone using EOS® (the Entrepreneurial Operating System®)[3] or thinking about it. For managers at startups, mid-market companies, and scaleups who know their calendar is a disaster but don't know how to fix the thing.

---

[1] In EOS, the Visionary is typically the founding entrepreneur who sees the big picture, thinks strategically, and is tuned in to the future of the industry. Visionaries are strong with big relationships and culture but are not typically suited to the day-to-day details of operations. Learn more at EOSWorldwide.com.

[2] The Integrator in EOS is the person who harmoniously integrates the major functions of the business, runs the organization day to day, and is accountable for profit and loss. The Integrator translates the Visionary's ideas into execution and typically facilitates the Level 10 Meeting. Learn more at EOSWorldwide.com.

[3] EOS is a complete set of simple concepts and practical tools used by more than 250,000 companies to get better at three things: Vision, Traction, and Healthy. Created by Gino Wickman. Learn more at EOSWorldwide.com.

And for anyone who's ever said, "We've got too many meetings," and wondered if there's a better way. (Spoiler: There is.)

Before you start rolling your eyes and thinking "yeah, right," this isn't just another book about meetings. There are plenty of those already.

This book is different because it is built on EOS, a proven operating system used by hundreds of thousands of companies to run their businesses. EOS gives you the structure, the tools, and the language to turn meetings from time-wasters into the most productive hours of your week.

And different because this is real. Not theory from a consultant who's never been in the trenches. This is from someone who's built companies, coached leadership teams through growth and crisis, and seen firsthand what happens when meetings work and when they don't.

You'll get stories. Real ones. Funny ones. Painful ones. The kinds that make you go, "Oh god, we do this." And you'll get practical tactics to use immediately. Not "try this if you feel like doing this," but processes with immediate results when you do the work.

The Problem We're Solving

Meetings are everywhere. They're on your calendar right now, stacked back-to-back. Some you scheduled. Some appeared like calendar gremlins. And if you're honest, you'd cancel at least half of them if you had the option.

The problem isn't that we meet too much (though we do). The problem is that most meetings don't accomplish anything. They're status updates disguised as strategy sessions. They're discussions that never turn into decisions. They're hour-long exercises where everyone is talking past each other until time runs out and someone says, "Let's circle back next week."

No one likes to say this out loud, but bad meetings don't waste time only. They come at a cost. They kill morale. They send a signal that this company doesn't know what they're doing. And over time, this compounds.

Good people check out. They stop contributing, stop engaging, and eventually stop showing up. Because it's tough to stay invested in something not going anywhere.

The EOS Solution

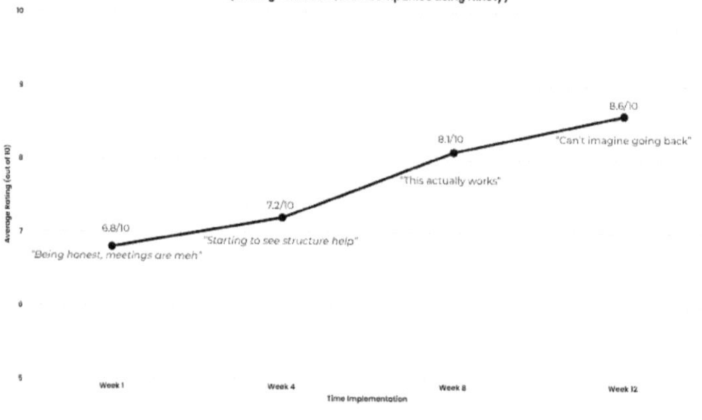

This book is built around principles from EOS, the Entrepreneurial Operating System. You don't need to be using EOS or know anything about it to benefit from what follows, but it helps to know the basics of what it is. EOS is a set of tools and disciplines helping leadership teams get clear on where they're going, build the right team, and create working processes.

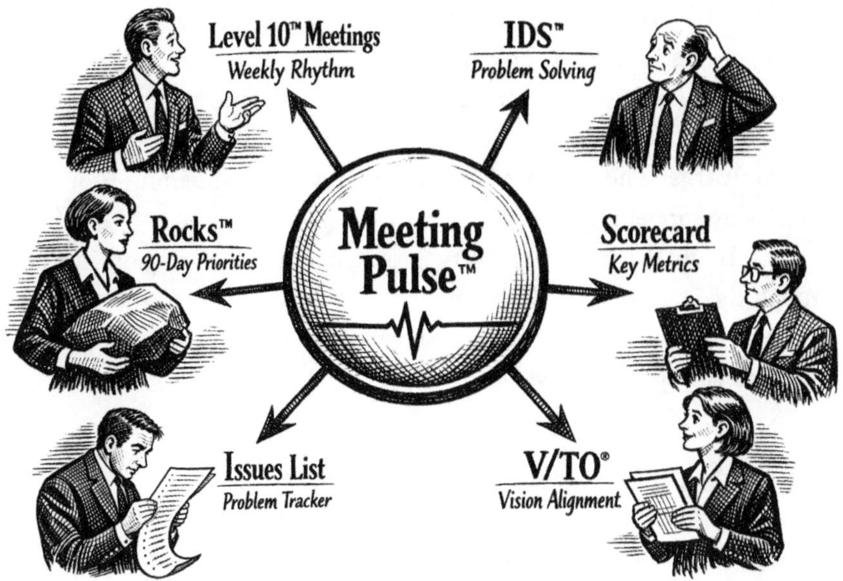

And at the center of EOS is The Meeting Pulse: the rhythm and structure that transforms meetings from chaos into clarity.

When you are Running on EOS®, you don't wing your meetings. You have a format. You have roles. You have a process for making decisions. You have a way to track what matters, solve problems, and hold people accountable. And most importantly, you have a shared language everyone on the team speaks.

This is not generic meeting advice. This system will give you the specific tools, formats, and disciplines to make EOS meetings work.

You'll learn about:

Level 10 Meetings®: The weekly rhythm keeping teams aligned and moving forward[4]

---

[4]   The Level 10 Meeting is a weekly, 90-minute structured meeting within EOS designed to keep leadership teams aligned, accountable, and focused on execution. Named for the 1-to-10 rating scale teams use to score each meeting. Learn more at EOSWorldwide.com/Blog/The-Level-10-Meeting

IDS® (Identify, Discuss, Solve): The process for cutting through decision fog and solving problems[5]

Rocks: The 90-day priorities that keep everyone focused on what matters[6]

Scorecards: The numbers showing you what's happening (not what you hope is happening)[7]

The Issues List: Where every problem is tracked so nothing falls through the cracks[8]

These aren't nice-to-haves. They're the foundation of how high-performing teams operate.

What You'll Get from This Book

This isn't a book to read once and then put on a shelf. It's a field guide. Something you reference. Something you share with your team. Something to help you fix your meetings starting today.

Each chapter tackles a specific problem:

- Why meetings suck and what to do about them

- How decision fatigue is killing your momentum

---

[5]   IDS stands for Identify, Discuss, Solve. IDS is the issue-solving process used in EOS Level 10 Meetings where teams identify the root cause of an issue, discuss the issue until clarity is reached, then solve with a concrete decision and action items. Learn more at EOSWorldwide.com.

[6]   Rocks are 90-day priorities within EOS. A company typically sets three to seven Rocks per quarter representing the most important things to accomplish. The concept originates from Stephen Covey's analogy of fitting rocks, pebbles, and sand in a jar. Learn more at EOSWorldwide.com.

[7]   The EOS Scorecard is a weekly tracking tool containing five to fifteen activity-based numbers (called Measurables) giving leadership teams a pulse on business performance. Displayed with thirteen weeks of history to identify patterns and trends. Learn more at EOSWorldwide.com.

[8]   The Issues List is a running log of all problems, ideas, and concerns to be addressed in the IDS portion of a Level 10 Meeting. Issues are captured throughout the week and prioritized at the start of each IDS session. Learn more at EOSWorldwide.com.

- Who's running the meeting (and why this matters)
- How to stop wasting time on fake productivity
- What to do when your presence as a leader shuts everyone down
- How to rebuild meeting culture after a crisis
- How to perform a Calendar Audit

And at the end of each chapter, you'll get a "Meetings Suck Less Realization." A simple takeaway to apply immediately.

A Note on Tone

This book is written the way I talk. Direct. Sometimes funny. Occasionally challenging. Because real conversations happen this way. I'm not interested in corporate-speak or theory for theory's sake. I'm interested in what works so we win.

Win. That's the word.

At Ninety, where I serve as Chief Revenue Officer and where we build the software helping thousands of companies run on business operating systems like EOS, we talk about winning all the time. We play to win the week, to win the quarter, to win the year. Not "participate in" the week. Not "survive" the quarter. Win.

Your meetings are where you find out if you're winning.

Most teams treat meetings like status updates. "Here's what happened." "Here's what I'm working on." That's reporting. Not winning.

Winning teams use meetings differently. They ask: Are we hitting our numbers? Are we making progress on the things we said mattered? Where are we stuck? What needs to change? And then they solve the thing. Right there. In the meeting.

The week is the unit of work. You win the week, or you don't. String together enough winning weeks, and you win the quarter. Win enough quarters, and you win the year. This is how momentum builds.

But you need to know if you're winning. Weekly. EOS gives you that cadence. The Meeting Pulse and the Level 10 Meeting show you the truth every seven days. No hiding. No spinning. You see the numbers. You face the issues. You make the adjustments.

This is what separates teams that grow from teams that grind.

You'll get stories from my own experience. Both the wins and the learnings. You'll hear about clients I've coached. And you'll get the kind of straight talk you'd get if we were sitting in a session room together, figuring out how to fix your business.

If you want polished and safe, there are other books for that. This one is for people who want real answers. For people who want to win.

My Background (And Why You Should Listen)

I'm a Professional EOS Implementer®. I've worked with more than 50 clients and hosted over 400 session days. I've seen what happens when companies implement EOS and commit to the discipline. And I've seen what happens when they don't.

Before coaching, I spent twenty-two years building entrepreneurial tech companies. I've been the Visionary, scrambling to figure things out. I've been the leader, making bad calls and learning from them. I've had wins and spectacular failures. And all of this taught me that systems, structure, and discipline matter.

These days, I split my time between two organizations: Impact Architects, a growth advisory firm I founded in 2018, and Ninety, the software helping organizations run on EOS. I coach several days a week, which keeps me grounded in what's happening in real companies. Not what consultants think should happen.

I've also been active in the entrepreneurial community. Former EO Cleveland member for thirteen years. Past Ernst & Young Entrepreneur of the Year winner. Board member and investor in SaaS companies in growth phases. I'm in the thick of this, like you.

My philosophy is to position what I do as a painkiller, not a vitamin. Vitamins are nice, and they might help eventually, but painkillers solve urgent problems now. So here's the painkiller for your meeting problem:

Read this front to back. Or skip to the chapter addressing your biggest pain point right now. Each chapter stands alone.

Regardless of which adventure you choose, I'd recommend you start with Chapter 1 and Chapter 2. They lay the foundation for everything else. Then pick the chapters speaking to where you're stuck.

And don't read only. Use this. Try the tools. Run a Level 10 Meeting. Rate your meetings. Track what changes. Embrace the messiness that comes with starting to change things. Share the realizations with your team. And when this works, my ask is for you to pass the book on to others. New or previously owned, doesn't matter to me, but the ripple impact of what works is important.

One Last Thing Before We Start

Meetings don't have to suck. I know they do right now. I know you're drowning in them, and they feel like a necessary evil.

But they're not. They're the place where strategy, execution, and culture come together. They're where decisions get made, problems get solved, and teams build trust. And when you get them right, they become the most valuable hours of your week.

This is what we're going for. Not perfection, but progress. Meetings that don't drain your soul. Meetings moving the business forward. Meetings making people say, "We used our time well." And how do we know? Because we rate *every* meeting on a scale of 1 to 10.

Let's get after this.

Before we begin, take a second to scan the QR code below. You'll find book bonuses, information on Ninety software, and additional resources to enhance your experience as you read.

Ninety.io/Meetings-Kinda-Suck

THIS COULD HAVE BEEN AN EMAIL... AND OTHER CRIMES AGAINST TIME

Most meetings suck.

Somewhere between the invention of the Outlook calendar and the first Zoom link, we forgot that meetings are supposed to do something. Aren't decisions, alignment, and progress the whole point? But instead, we get agenda-less calendar gremlins, vague action items (if any), and enough buzzwords to make a thesaurus weep. There's a reason the idea of "This meeting was an email" has been a trending topic on social media. And if you've ever sat through a meeting and had this exact thought, congratulations. You're part of a club spanning industries, time zones, and generations.

Let's look at how we got here, why we're still here, and how EOS helps us get the hell out.

The Cultural History of Meeting Mayhem

It didn't start out broken. There was a time when meetings were sacred. You gathered the tribe, broke bread (or stale pastries), and made decisions. You aligned. You rallied. You moved. The theory.

Then came the calendar invites. The recurring ones. The "weekly touch base." The "quick sync." The "let's circle back." With technology came the ability to put recurring meetings on autopilot. Meetings multiplied like rabbits, and nobody bothered to ask if they served a purpose. We convinced ourselves because the meeting was on the calendar, we didn't have the authority to question whether or not it was needed, and being busy in meetings meant we were doing important work. Spoiler: not.

I've spent twenty-two years building companies, and I've sat through my share of terrible meetings. Early on, I thought this was part of the game. Like paying taxes or pretending to care about the Super Bowl when you don't follow football. But then I started coaching leadership teams, and I realized the problem isn't people hating meetings. People hate bad meetings. And bad meetings are everywhere because nobody taught us how to run good ones.

Raise your hand if you took a "How to Run Efficient Meetings" class in high school. Obviously, I don't see how many of you are raising your hands, but my guess is slim to none. Things like meeting agendas, solving real problems in real time, and actionable takeaways are things we're supposed to figure out on our own, preferably while also hitting quarterly targets and not losing our minds.

The Five Deadly Sins of Meetings

Let's name the culprits. Here's what makes a meeting suck:

1. No Clear Purpose

Ever get a meeting invite saying "Weekly Sync" with zero context? Cool. So you show up, and someone says, "I figured we'd see what's going on?" Not a meeting. A hostage situation.

If you don't articulate why people need to be in the room, don't put them there. Simple.

We say every great meeting has a clear objective, an aligned agenda, and the discipline to win. We are objective-focused, not agenda-led. Be prepared to speak up if it's not working to create value. The aligned agenda serves that objective. That's staying focused when things get messy.

If Issue #3 turns out to be the real problem, we don't march through Issues #1 and #2 just because they're on the list. We go where the value lives.

2. No Prep

Here's a classic: ten people show up, and the first fifteen minutes are spent figuring out what we're even talking about. Someone scrambles to pull up a doc. Someone else didn't read what was sent. And now we're all trapped in a performance of "let's figure this out live."

Prep isn't optional. Prep is respect.

Prep isn't optional. Prep is respect. For everyone's time. For the work. For the idea, "Maybe, we get something done today."

3. No Decisions

Ever leave a meeting and ask, "So... what did we decide?" This question is the smoke signal of a wasted hour. Talk happened. Words were exchanged. Nothing changed.

If you have the same conversation more than twice without solving anything, you're not meeting. You're loitering.

4. Too Many People

More isn't merrier. More is murky. Ten people in a room equals ten different ideas of what was decided. And at least one person wondering if they were invited by mistake.

Ever sat in a meeting where you didn't say a word for an hour? You're not alone. Meetings are expensive. If you wouldn't pay $2,000 for this hour, why did you invite ten salaried people?

5. No Accountability

Here's the thing about accountability: someone needs to own the meeting. Someone needs to facilitate the thing. Someone needs to capture what gets decided. These are three different jobs.

Owner. Facilitator. Note Taker.

You need all three, minimum. Can one person do them all? Sure. But not well. Not when the meeting gets hard.

EOS starts with two roles: the person leading the meeting and the person taking notes. This works. I've built on this foundation by splitting the leader role into two distinct jobs: Owner and Facilitator. Why? Because after hundreds of sessions, I've watched people try to own the objective while also managing the room, and something often gets dropped. Separating these roles makes both stronger.

The Owner sets the objective. Why are we here? What needs to happen? The Owner invites the right people. The Owner makes sure the meeting matters.

The Facilitator keeps things moving. Pulls people in. Calls out patterns. Manages the time. Redirects when the group wanders. The Facilitator serves the objective.

The Note Taker captures decisions, to-dos, and who owns what. Without this, everyone leaves with different versions of what happened. And next week, nobody remembers who agreed to do the thing.

Three roles. You need them all.

Now, here's where meetings fall apart. Someone tries to be all three at once. The owner is facilitating while trying to remember what was decided. Or the facilitator is taking notes while trying to manage the conversation. Or nobody takes notes at all because everyone assumes someone else is.

When you have many people in meetings, people assume someone else will take the lead. But at the end of the meeting, there is no clear RACI (responsible, accountable, consulted, informed). Everyone looks at everyone else, assuming things are handled. But often in the meetings, you never established who is taking on what.

Let's say someone volunteers to "take this." Great! Except they don't. The same topic reappears like a bad penny next week. Cue the déjà vu. Again.

And let's be honest: people say, "I'll take this," but they mean, "I'll forget about this the moment I hang up." Accountability only works when there's visibility. Without clear roles in the meeting, without someone capturing who owns what, without follow-through, you get the same conversations over and over.

EOS Scorecards make things visible. The To-Dos make commitments clear. The Issues capture what needs solving. But first, you need the three roles. Owner. Facilitator. Note Taker.

For a quick huddle, it might be fine for one person to be all three, but it's not fine for anything where decisions matter. Not fine for anything requiring follow-through.

So before your next meeting, ask: Who owns this meeting? Who's facilitating? Who's taking notes? If you don't have clear answers, you don't have accountability. And without accountability, you're just talking.

The Emotional Cost of a Bad Meeting

When a meeting goes bad, wasted time is only one of the costs. Everyone loses morale. Every pointless conversation chips away at trust, energy, and buy-in. Leaders lose credibility. Teams lose patience. Before long, the eye rolls start before the call even connects.

Once this happens, people start treating meetings like weather: something they have to get through. They stop bringing ideas. They stop speaking up. And eventually, they stop showing up altogether. "Sorry, double-booked" becomes code for "I won't sit through another hour of nonsense."

Multiply this by fifty-two weeks. Multiply by every department. Add in the side effects: anxiety, disengagement, apathy. And boom, your company culture got a little bit sicker.

Still think your meetings are "fine"?

You know what gets me? We track every dollar, make budgets, and stress over the bottom line, but we treat time like it's free. We fill calendars with hour-long meetings that never accomplish much and wonder why we're all exhausted.

Time is the only truly finite resource. You can raise more capital. You can hire more people. You can't manufacture more hours. And yet, we act like meetings are free. They're not.

Time is the only truly finite resource.

Do the math. Ten people in a meeting for an hour. If the average salary in the room is $100K, that comes to roughly $500 in labor cost right there. Multiply by every pointless meeting your company runs in a week. Then a month. Then a year. Adds up fast.

What about the opportunity cost? The work not getting done? The ideas not getting explored? The momentum dying while everyone sits in a conference room nodding politely?

When I work with leadership teams, one of the first things we do is audit their calendar. Not because I'm some efficiency nerd (okay, a little), but because this reveals where the business is bleeding time. And nine times out of ten, it's meetings. Meetings that don't need to happen. Meetings that take too long. Meetings where nobody knows why they're there.

The Calendar Audit[IP] (Yes, You Need One)

This typically comes up when we roll out EOS. The calendar audit connects directly to your Delegate and Elevate® work. This EOS tool helps you figure out what you should be doing, what you need to delegate, and what you need to eliminate entirely.[9] Your calendar shows you the truth about how you're spending your time.

Here's what I have people do. Pull up your calendar for the last month. Look at every recurring meeting. Ask three questions:

- What problem does this meeting solve?
- Is this problem still a problem?
- Is this meeting solving the problem?

You'll kill at least 30 percent of your meetings immediately. Another 30 percent need to be consolidated. The rest need structure.

But here's the thing. You don't have to do this manually anymore. Tools like Google Gemini can audit your calendar for you. Give the thing access to your calendar and ask for a breakdown. It'll tell you how much time you spent in meetings, how many had objectives or agendas, and how many were deep work versus interrupt work versus wellness time.

I started doing this for myself. My workout time is on the calendar. So is my Rock time (the hours I protect for getting my priorities done). Gemini calculates how much time I spent on each category. Shows me patterns. Tells me when I'm slipping.

The data is brutal. And useful.

You see where you're spending your time versus where you think you're spending your time. Most leaders are shocked. "I thought I was focused on strategic work." Nope. You're in status update meetings fifteen hours a week.

The AI can also spot meetings without objectives. No agenda. No clear purpose. These are the first ones to kill or fix.

Here's what you do. Run the audit. Get the data. Then ask yourself: Does this calendar reflect the person I need to be for this company to win?

If the answer is no, you've got work to do.

---

[9]   Delegate and Elevate is an EOS tool helping leaders identify work they love and are great at versus work to delegate. Activities are sorted into four quadrants based on enjoyment and ability, with the goal of spending the most time in the "love it and great at it" quadrant. Learn more at EOSWorldwide.com/Delegate-and-Elevate.

Protect Your Time Like You Protect Your Money

Once you see where your time is going, protect the things that matter. Block your calendar for Rock time. The work driving your priorities forward. Protect this like you'd protect a meeting with your biggest customer. Because this is more important.

Schedule your wellness time. Your workout. Your think time. Your family time. Put these things on the calendar. Otherwise, meetings will eat it all.

And for meetings you keep, add structure. Every meeting needs an objective. Every invite needs an agenda. If you're inviting someone to a meeting and you don't have a clear objective, you're wasting their time. Don't send the invite.

Does the thought of me auditing your calendar make your stomach drop? Then you already know this problem needs to be fixed.

10 team members x **100,000** salary x **1** hour = **$500**

Enter EOS: A System, Not a Suggestion

EOS doesn't fix meetings by telling you to "try harder." It fundamentally changes the game. Hands you the playbook. With rules. With roles. With tools, turning time into Traction®.[10]

And starts with four heavy hitters:

1. Level 10 Meetings

Not a weekly check-in. A disciplined format. A focused hour where issues don't get discussed, but they get solved.

---

[10] Traction is one of the Six Key Components® of the EOS Model®, describing the focus, discipline, and accountability necessary to achieve your Vision. Also the title of Gino Wickman's foundational book on EOS. Learn more at EOSWorldwide.com.

The structure matters. You walk in knowing the agenda. You walk out knowing the actions. Not magic. Muscle memory. And when done right, it becomes the most valuable hour of the week.[11]

2. Rocks

No more vague goals. Rocks are the 90-day priorities moving the business. When you know your Rocks, you stop wasting meetings chasing squirrels.

Rocks give you context. They help you filter. They answer, "Is this issue even worth talking about right now?

3. Scorecards

It's hard to argue about feelings when you've got numbers. Scorecards make performance visible. Measurable. Actionable. Meetings become check-ins on reality, not debates on memory.

---

[11]   To learn more about the L10 Agenda and how to run the meeting, go to EOSWorldwide.com/Level-10.

They also kill the passive-aggressive vibe. Nobody has to guess how marketing is doing. The data speaks. Loudly.

4. Issues List

Every lingering "thing we need to talk about" goes here. Captured. Named. Prioritized. And attacked with IDS®: Identify, Discuss, Solve.

No more circling the drain. No more punting to next week. Problems turning into progress. One issue at a time.

What We Talk About When We Talk About Meetings

There are two kinds of companies: Companies that run meetings and companies where meetings run them.

In EOS, meetings are part of the operating system. Not a necessary evil. They're where strategy, people, and execution meet. But only if you stop letting meetings become a dumping ground for updates, sidebars, and invisible decisions.

Here's the shift: every meeting must earn the spot. EOS helps you demand more from your calendar. And more from the people in the room.

Let's compare two sales teams. Same industry. Same tools. Same revenue target.

Team A:

- Meets weekly.
- No agenda.
- Talks in circles.
- Everyone leaves more confused than when they came in.

Team B:

- Meets weekly.
- Uses the Level 10 Meeting format.
- Scorecard shows they're off track.
- They IDS the root issue in twenty minutes.
- Leave with one decision, three to-dos, and a sense of progress.

Which team hits quota? You already know.

I've seen this play out across hundreds of companies. The pattern holds. The meeting discipline pays off.

Making the Shift

If your meetings feel painful now, you don't need to blow everything up. You need to anchor in a few working practices.

Start small. Try one Level 10 Meeting format with one team. Track how this feels. Track what gets solved. Track how many side conversations evaporate.

Talk to your team. Ask them:

- What's the most valuable meeting you attend each week?
- What's the one meeting you wish we'd cancel?
- What meeting helps you do your job better?

Then listen. They'll tell you the truth if you're brave enough to ask. Before we wrap this chapter, let's recap what makes a meeting suck:

- No clear purpose
- No prep
- No decisions
- Too many people
- No accountability

And what EOS brings to the table:

- A weekly rhythm (Level 10)
- A scoreboard everyone sees (Scorecard)
- Rocks to prioritize
- Issues List to attack what matters

If you're nodding along because that first list sounds like the meetings you hate, good. You're not alone. And you're not stuck.

Most teams don't need more meetings. They need better ones.

"Meetings Suck Less" Realization

Every complaint about a meeting is a complaint about missing structure. EOS gives your meetings structure. Structure gives you your time and sanity back.

Next up: Let's talk about the hidden culprit behind your meeting dread. Not what you think. (Unless you guessed decision fatigue. In which case, you're ahead of the class.)

MEETING RED FLAG BINGO 

NO AGENDA	"LET'S TAKE THIS OFFLINE"	LONG MONOLOGUE
WHO'S TAKING NOTES?	AWKWARD SILENCE	TANGENT
"I'LL FOLLOW UP"	FREE SPACE	DISCONNECTED CALL
REPEATS SAME POINT	BRAINSTORMING SESSION	LET'S TABLE THAT
LATE JOINER	TECH ISSUES	ON MUTE

Want to know if your meetings are broken? Here's a simple diagnostic. We made a bingo card. If you get three in a row during your next meeting, you've got work to do.

2

"LET'S CIRCLE BACK... TO THE REAL PROBLEM"

We don't need to reinvent the wheel to fix meetings. We need to figure out why the thing keeps spinning in place without going anywhere. Most of the time, the wheel isn't stuck because people are lazy or disengaged. It gets stuck because no one made a decision. Welcome to the underbelly of meeting fatigue: decision fatigue.

The Meeting Doom Loop

Back in 2002, I read *Good to Great* by Jim Collins. It changed how I think about business. One concept stuck with me: the Flywheel versus the Doom Loop.

Collins showed how great companies build momentum through consistent effort. They push the flywheel. Week after week, they do the disciplined things. Over time, the wheel spins faster. Less effort, more momentum. Breakthrough becomes inevitable.

The Doom Loop is different. Companies skip the buildup. They chase the quick win, the big pivot, the magic bullet. Something goes wrong, so they react. They call the emergency meeting. They shift direction. Nobody follows through because there's no rhythm. No cadence. The energy dies. Another disappointment hits. The cycle repeats.[12]

---

[12] Collins, Jim. *Good to Great: Why Some Companies Make the Leap... and Others Don't.* Harper Business, 2001.

Most companies live in the Doom Loop without knowing it.

I lived there for years. I built my first company by calling "emergency strategy sessions" every time we missed a number. We'd get fired up, make new commitments, and then... nothing. No follow-through. No cadence. I thought I was being responsive. Agile. Adaptive. I was feeding the loop. My team got whiplash from all the direction changes. Took me longer than I'd like to admit to figure this out.

Your meetings are either pushing your flywheel forward or they're feeding the loop.

And here's what I've learned after two decades building companies and coaching leadership teams: the Doom Loop lives in your meetings.

Your meetings are either pushing your flywheel forward or they're feeding the loop. There's no middle ground.

Let me show you what I mean.

The Doom Loop: Why Your Meetings Suck

You've been here. A project tanks. Numbers miss. A customer complains. Leadership freaks out.

Someone calls a meeting. "We need to get aligned." "We need to pivot." "We need to figure this out."

Everyone shows up. You spend an hour talking. People leave feeling energized. Finally, we're fixing this thing. Then what happens? Nothing. No follow-up. No accountability. No rhythm to check back in. The energy fades. Work gets in the way. The urgency disappears.

Three weeks later, the same problem shows up again. Rinse and repeat. This is the Meeting Doom Loop.

Here's how the thing works:

1. Disappointment hits. Something breaks. A goal gets missed. A deadline slips.

2. The reaction comes. Leadership calls the "big meeting" to fix things. Now.

3. The false start happens. People leave feeling good, but it only lasts about 24 hours. You get the "Great meeting!" Slack messages. Everyone's aligned. This time will be different. (Narrator: This time was not different.)

4. The drift begins. No cadence. No pulse. The energy disappears. People forget.

5. The result arrives. Another disappointment. Back to step one.

Why does this suck? Because you're spinning your wheels. Every meeting is a new direction. Zero net momentum. Your team knows things. They see the pattern. They stop trusting the meetings. They stop believing the decisions will stick.

You've taught them that meetings are where we talk, not where we move.

The Meeting Flywheel: How to Build Momentum

The Flywheel is different. You have disciplined people in the room. You confront brutal facts every week. You execute with rhythm.

You don't swing for the fences. You push the wheel. One more turn. Same cadence, same structure, same accountability.

Over time, the wheel spins faster. Decisions get easier. Problems get solved before they explode. The team trusts the process. Momentum builds.

Here's what the Flywheel looks like in practice:

Step 1: Get the right people in the room. Your leadership team. The council. The people who own the outcomes.

Step 2: Confront the brutal facts. Every week. Identify issues and address them. No hiding. No sugar-coating.

Step 3: Execute the meeting with regularity. Don't skip the thing. Show up. Work the structure. The rhythm matters more than the energy.

Step 4: Let the momentum build until the breakthrough comes. You don't have to push as hard. The cadence carries you. Information flows. Accountability sticks.

This is the difference between reacting and building.

Doom vs. Fly

Let me break this down. Here's what the Doom Loop looks like compared to the Flywheel:

Doom Loop:

- Goal: React to the crisis of the day
- The Push: Inconsistent and jerky
- Reality Check: Hiding the brutal facts to save face
- New Initiatives: "The new meeting" as a last-ditch fallback
- Feeling: Exhaustion and meeting fatigue

Meeting Flywheel:

- Goal: Push the flywheel one more turn
- The Push: Rhythmic and synchronized
- Reality Check: Confront the true state of things every week with data
- New Initiatives: "The existing cadence" as a consistent guide
- Feeling: Traction and momentum

The Doom Loop feels like work. The Flywheel feels like progress.

Here's the hard truth. Most leadership teams are stuck in the loop. They don't want to be there. They work hard. They care about the business. But they've never built the rhythm.

They've confused activity with progress. Meetings with momentum. They've got forty-seven recurring meetings on the calendar and somehow still feel like nothing gets done. (Because nothing does.)

I've seen this play out dozens of times. Smart people. Good intentions. Bad meetings. They keep calling emergency sessions. They keep looking for the breakthrough moment. They keep hoping the next pivot will be the one.

But breakthrough doesn't come from pivots. Breakthrough comes from the push. The consistent, disciplined, rhythmic push on the flywheel.

Your meetings are the push.

When you treat your meeting cadence as the rhythmic push on your company's flywheel, you stop "having meetings" and start building momentum.

Are you ready to make that shift?

You're going to learn how to build The Meeting Pulse®.[13] How to structure meetings that work. How to get your team to trust the process. How to push the flywheel instead of feeding the loop.

You're going to see what happens when meetings become the heartbeat of your business, not the time suck. You're going to feel what momentum feels like. Let's get to work.

The Loop in Action

You've seen this. A project misses the mark. Numbers slip. A customer complains. Someone calls a meeting to fix things. Everyone shows up. You spend an hour talking. People leave energized. "Finally, we're addressing this."

Then what happens? Nothing. No decision. No clear owner. No follow-through. The energy fades.

Three weeks later, same issue comes back. You discuss the thing again. Different words, same outcome. The wheel spins. You go nowhere.

This is the Doom Loop in real time. This is the actual pattern killing your momentum.

The Flywheel needs decisions to spin. Every decision you make pushes the wheel forward. Another turn. More momentum. But when you leave meetings without deciding, you're not pushing anything. You're feeding the loop.

---

[13]   The Meeting Pulse is the EOS method for keeping teams connected through a consistent meeting rhythm: weekly Level 10 Meetings, quarterly planning sessions, and annual planning sessions. Same day, same time, same agenda. Learn more at EOSWorldwide.com.

And here's a not-so-fun fact: most teams don't realize they're stuck until someone points out the friction. You think you're being thoughtful. Collaborative. Careful. In truth, you're avoiding.

Death by a Thousand "What Should We Do?"

Ever left a meeting more confused than when you walked in? Join the club. You've got ten smart people, each tossing ideas around like open mic night at the TEDx bar. Lots of opinions. Lots of nodding. A

deck with pie charts. But when the room clears? No decisions. Another meeting on the calendar to "circle back."

This is decision fatigue at work. The meeting didn't suck because people didn't care. It sucked because no one steered the ship. The fog of "Should we? Would we? Might we?" kills momentum faster than a faulty Wi-Fi connection on Zoom.

Here's what happens when you don't decide. First, you waste the time spent in the meeting. Second, you waste the week between meetings while the problem festers. Third, your team stops trusting decisions will stick. They start hedging. They wait to see which way the wind blows before **Indecision is a decision.** committing. Trust erodes.

The thing is, indecision is a decision. You decided to let the problem continue. You decided to avoid the hard conversation. You decided momentum doesn't matter as much as comfort.

Every unmade decision feeds the Doom Loop. Every decision made pushes the Flywheel.

In EOS companies, we call this out for what it is: a lack of clarity. And we fix the thing with tools designed exactly for this problem.

The Flywheel Needs Fuel

The Flywheel runs on decisions. Not perfect decisions. Not easy decisions. Just decisions.

When you decide, you create momentum. The team knows what to do. They go execute. You check progress next week. You make adjustments. The wheel keeps spinning.

When you don't decide, you create friction. The team doesn't know what to do. They wait. They guess. They work on the wrong things. The wheel stops.

Most leadership teams think they need better ideas. Better strategy. Better execution. What they need is better decision-making and the discipline to work through an issue until something gets decided. Then move on.

This is what IDS does. Identify the real issue. Discuss until everyone's clear. Solve the thing with a concrete decision and clear ownership. Not, "Let's think about this." Not, "Let's explore options." Solve.

One decision. One push on the wheel. Do this every week. The momentum builds. This chapter is about breaking the loop. About making meetings productive by making decisions. About pushing the Flywheel instead of spinning your wheels. Let me show you how.

The Five Whats That Never Get an Answer

Early in my coaching career, I worked with a team swearing they ran productive meetings. They were bought into EOS, but they had their own twist on things. They'd discovered this technique. Asking "what?" five times to get to the root of an issue. Sounded smart in theory. In practice? A disaster.

I watched them facilitate an issue during a quarterly session. The facilitator kept asking, "Okay, so then what?" And then, "Now what?" And then, "What about this?" Thirty minutes in, they were still spinning. Only three of the seven people in the room were even engaged. The extroverts had sucked all the oxygen out, and the introverts had no idea how to break in. There was no structure. There was only a facilitator asking endless "what" questions while everyone else slowly lost the will to live.

Finally, I called timeout. "Alright, let's pause. Who thinks this is productive? Raise your hand."

Only the integrator raised his hand. The guy who was facilitating the whole thing. Everyone else? They knew this was a mess.

I asked if they'd let me try my way. Ten minutes later, using IDS, we had a solve everyone aligned with. The relief in the room was palpable. One person said, "Yeah, this is so much better. Let's follow the process."

Here's the thing about IDS. It's not meant to be emotionally satisfying. You're going to want to say things that feel urgent in the moment but aren't actually relevant. I'm going to ask you not to. You're going to want to politick because you believe passionately in something. I'm going to ask you not to. We're going to lean into the structure, and you're going to find this productive. Because with seven people in a room making the kind of money we're paying them, we need to be productive.

The EOS Antidote: IDS and the Decision-Making Muscle

IDS stands for Identify, Discuss, and Solve. This tool is the scalpel we use to cut through decision fog. Here's the trick: don't jump to solving. Start by naming the real issue. If you're arguing about symptoms, you're wasting your breath.

IDS can't be just theory. It must become muscle memory. Once your team speaks the IDS language fluently, meetings become sharp. Focused. Energized. You get things done.

Start by naming the real issue.

Let me break this down:

Identify: Figure out what's going on. Don't stop at the surface problem. Get to the root. If sales are down, ask whether this is lead quality, pricing, your sales process, or team capacity. Name the thing and get specific.

And here's where most teams skip a critical step. I call it "who-who-one-what." The first "who" is "Who's the right owner?" When an issue shows up, identify who should own the thing. The second "who" is "Who's involved?" This matters because if this person isn't in the meeting, that's not cool. Or if I'm bringing an issue about you to the team and we haven't talked first, again, uncool. Sometimes when we catch this second "who," I'll say, "Alright, you two go talk. I'm giving you a to-do. Come back next week if this is still an issue. But you should talk first."

At Ninety, we have a philosophy called Succeed or Escalate[IP]: Try to solve the thing at the lowest level. If you don't, then escalate to the team.

The "one" is one sentence of three to five words, but no more than seven. I'll let someone go for a minute when they raise an issue, but then I compress their thoughts down to one sentence. This forces clarity.

The "what" is "What do you think is the outcome we get done in this meeting?" Not next quarter. Not eventually. Right now, in this time period. What's the what?

Once you've got those four things clear, now you open things up for discussion.

Discuss: Once you know the issue, now you talk. But stay focused. You're not spinning in circles. You're exploring solutions, testing ideas, and bringing different perspectives to the table. This is where healthy conflict happens, and that's important.

Here's a practice I use when teams are struggling with going too long: time-boxing. Our software at Ninety has a timer on the left-hand side. It doesn't ding, which is perfect. I'll say, "Hey team, we're going to time-box this at ten minutes. I'm going to throw a ten-minute timer up, and it's going to remind us when we hit ten. Doesn't mean we won't keep going. Means we're all going to be aware we've spent ten minutes on this, out of sixty minutes total. We need another 10. If we need another ten, I'll put it on the clock, and we'll go again."

This tool isn't EOS; it's just good time management. But it keeps us from getting lost in an issue.

Solve: Make a decision, assign ownership, and set a deadline. Then move on. No "let's think about this" or "we'll revisit later." Decide and keep moving.

Now, what if you don't get to solve? Then we're going to need forward progress. "Alright team, sounds like we didn't find the solve. We probably need additional information from a third party outside the company. So we're going to take a to-do on this. Who owns the to-do? Great, Kris owns the thing. He's going to go figure out what else we need, and he'll come back next week better prepared."

Here's where things get interesting: Say I do this work and realize, "Oh man, obvious solve." I'm not bringing this back as an issue. I'm going to turn it into a headline in our world. Now I'm informing everyone of what happened rather than coming back to it as an issue again. If someone hears my headline and goes, "Hey, I still have an issue with this," cool. It's now an issue again. And by the way, the ownership will most likely shift. Because if this is your issue now, you're the issue owner.

The beauty of IDS is how it forces discipline. You don't hide behind vague language. You don't punt indefinitely. The process demands progress.

When Everyone's Talking, but No One Decides

Teams constantly talking without deciding aren't broken. They're stuck. Stuck in fear of conflict, of being wrong, of accountability.

EOS doesn't eliminate tension. It channels the tension by giving people structure, a shared language, and a rhythm for making calls. You start solving real problems, not discussing them. Every unmade decision is a tax on morale, speed, and trust.

I was at an ENRG meeting this morning. These are community groups that have exploded around EOS in the last year. Fifty chapters now, growing like crazy. I spoke on Rocks today, and afterward, they did issue-solving. Everyone brought one issue.

They were spinning, like I described earlier. The facilitator, Carol, wasn't doing the who-who-one-what. I jumped in. "Hey Carol, you're not doing who-who-one-what. Is there a reason?" She said, "Yeah, I don't like the thing."

I said, "Huh. Because we don't know what this guy's issue is yet. And it's been ten minutes. We should try it."

Once we used the framework, everything clicked. That's the strength of structure.

What Decision Fatigue Looks Like

When you're facilitating (and by the way, we use the term "facilitator" and "scribe" in EOS, not "host"), you need to watch for the signs. Decision fatigue sounds like: "Ah, here we go again. We're on this again." People are exhausted because you're bringing up the same issue for the sixth time, and you're not getting to the core.

When you sense fatigue, stop the team. "Alright, let's try this again. We keep bringing this issue back because we haven't found the core issue. Let's dig a bit deeper."

Often, the core is a person problem. The elephant in the room. That conversation usually goes something like this: "Every time we try to solve this issue, it comes back to this one guy, and he's a jerk."

"Okay, so why isn't he gone?"

"He's a good performer. How can we fire him when he has 25 percent of our sales?"

"Well, we're going to be here again next week. Because he's only going to piss more people off."

The brilliant jerk moment. In these cases, there's always something underlying: an elephant in the room, a person issue, something structural stopping you from moving forward.

Here's a real example: I had a client who kept losing people in a territory. Why'd they lose Susie? They were forcing her to cover Indiana while she was covering Ohio, driving fifty miles every day. They should have hired somebody in Indiana. Now they've got to go replace Susie. A bad idea.

Customer concentration is another common elephant in the room. I probably come across ten clients a year who have one customer bringing in over 50 percent of their revenue when I start coaching them. This customer makes demands all the time. The company is scared because what happens if they go away? So this customer ends up on the issues list every single time. I did an annual with a client who finally fired the customer, taking 30 percent of their revenue out the door this year. They were losing employees because they were mistreating them in trying to over-serve this customer. They decided to take the hit.

A hard decision. But otherwise, every time I saw them, that client would have been on the issues list once again. I would ask, "What are you going to do about this?" Their answer would be, "Well, we're going to go have one more conversation with them." Yeah, but they're not going to stop. Another conversation won't change who they are or how they behave.

The Archive: Your Meeting History Lesson

One of the great features of Ninety is the archive. If, while I'm coaching, I sense us starting to spin on a repeat issue, I'll turn on the archive. "Okay, how many times have we talked about this?" They'll say, "Well, a few."

Then we go to the archive and type in the keyword. "Well, team, looks like this last quarter, this is the tenth time we've talked about this."

Promoting this awareness of repeat issues is one of the values of the software. Once I see what happened in the short term, I ask: "Is this solved, or should this be a long-term issue we need to do something different about so we don't have to keep talking about it?

The Data Trap

Data is another common factor in decision-making issues. People raise issues but don't have the data, so they say, "We're going to have to wait to make this decision because we need the data." Data is inherently messy at every company. Not moving because you don't have the data is not the best practice.

You've got to trust your gut. You've been doing this long enough, and the thing smells wrong. I tell our Visionary all the time: "You've got to trust our gut. If we're sitting here saying, 'But we don't have all the data,' I'm like, 'Yeah, but at some point, we've done this enough. If we don't move, we're going to take another quarter to go learn a lesson we already know the answer to.'"

Part of being a leader is making decisions and owning them. We're going to be wrong as leaders. We've got to own when we're wrong. But we also need to move. Businesses have a pace they need to maintain for forward trajectory, and waiting for better data when it might not be coming anytime soon gets us in trouble.

Part of being a leader is making decisions and owning them.

Analysis paralysis is real. Let's not do anything, wait for the data, and then two years down the road, you still don't have the data. Or you have the data, but now things have shifted, the market's going in a different direction, and you're left behind. You should have taken a step or done a little trial and error.

The Momentum Multiplier

Solve one meaningful issue per meeting. Fifty-two a year. If even half creates impact, you will see a tidal wave of progress.

1 decision/week = **52** decisions/year = **Massive Progress**

Momentum isn't built in big launches. It's built in consistent choices. Weekly. Deliberate. Practical.

When teams are high-performing, they track how many issues they solve. In Ninety, our software says: "How many issues did you solve last week? How many did you solve this week?" There's no right answer because some are more strategic than others. But on average, high-performing teams are addressing four to six issues every week.

From Ideas to Commitments: Why Rocks Matter

Ever had a meeting where everyone agreed on an idea, but nothing happened? Because there was no container. No Rock. No commitment.

Rocks send a clear message: this matters, deserves time, and will get done.

They also force prioritization. Not everything gets to be a Rock. Choosing them means saying no to noise, to distractions, to good ideas not being great.

When you know your Rocks, you stop wasting meetings chasing squirrels. Rocks give you context. They help you filter. They answer the question, "Is this issue even worth talking about right now?" If the thing doesn't tie to a Rock or a critical company priority, it must wait.

What Happens When You Don't Decide

Let's talk consequences. Delays pile up. Teams lose steam. Customers notice. Morale dips. Smart people start checking out.

One of the most expensive non-decisions I witnessed was during the pandemic. A business needed to pivot. Their whole model was in-person events and training. Overnight, gone. They weren't willing to do the scary, hard things. Their theory was, "Well, this won't last long. We'll pick the things back up when this turns around."

This is never a healthy approach to sudden change. What we did know is we didn't know how long this would last. So until you know, you should probably decide to have a secondary strategy versus taking a "wait and see" approach.

I saw another company go the opposite way. They laid off a ton of people because they panicked. Then their business was declared essential, and they wanted people to come back to work. But they didn't get them all back. People were pissed: "Forget this, I'm going to do something else." They went the wrong way with the decision.

The hard part? Some of these moments of indecision take different shapes over time. Since the first year I was at Ninety, I've been asking the same question: "Should this company have an Integrator? One person?" The issue came up again recently when I was talking with our CFO and Visionary in Park City, because our Visionary is trying to sit in three leadership seats at once. It's not a best operating practice. You can't do all of them well.

In situations like this, you're going to make critical business decisions, create theories, and try things that don't work, so you'll have to try again. One of my best long-term examples is a pricing and packaging issue. Ninety is on our fifth iteration. We realize something didn't work, so we go price and package all over again.

Another case of indecision: a landscaping company that delayed buying trucks for months. Once they IDSed the issue, they determined it wasn't about cost. The issue was trust. One leader didn't believe quotes were vetted. Once it all surfaced, the decision was made, and alignment followed.

A digital agency suffered campaign delays. IDS uncovered a broken onboarding process. They built a checklist. Deadlines improved. Teams got along better. Clients noticed.

These aren't unicorn stories. This is what happens when you create a system for making decisions. Problems feeling insurmountable become manageable. And meetings draining energy start generating the thing.

Deep Dive: EOS Tools for Killing Decision Fatigue

Let's get tactical. Here are the tools to make your decision-making easier:

1. The Accountability Chart®

   Clear roles prevent finger-pointing. This organizational chart shows who owns what. When an issue comes up, you know exactly who's responsible for solving the thing. No more "I thought you were handling this."[14]

2. The Issues List

   Everything goes here. Every problem. Every question. Every concern. Then you prioritize. You tackle the most important issues first. And you don't leave the meeting until they're solved.

3. The Vision/Traction Organizer® (V/TO®)

   This is your company's playbook. It answers the big questions: Where are we going? How are we getting there? What are our core values? What's our ten-year target? When everyone's aligned on these, smaller decisions become easier because you have a framework to evaluate them against.[15]

4. The 90-Day World®

   "EOS runs on 90-day cycles for a reason. Ninety days is long enough to get meaningful work done and short enough to keep your team honest about whether they did the work or not. Rocks create urgency. Quarterly planning creates rhythm. You're not trying to plan five years out (which is mostly fantasy anyway).

---

[14] The Accountability Chart is the EOS version of an organizational chart. Rather than focusing on titles and reporting lines, the chart defines seats based on the functions the business needs, with five major roles per seat and one accountable owner per seat. Learn more at EOSWorldwide.com/Blog/EOS-Accountability-Chart.

[15] The Vision/Traction Organizer (V/TO) is a two-page strategic plan answering eight key questions: Core Values, Core Focus, 10-Year Target, Marketing Strategy, 3-Year Picture, 1-Year Plan, Quarterly Rocks, and Issues List. Learn more at EOSWorldwide.com."

You're focusing on the next 90 days. What do we accomplish? What do we need to do to get there?[16]

The Hard Truth About Conflict

Here's something nobody wants to hear: if you're not having healthy conflict in your meetings, you're not making real decisions.

Healthy conflict is a sign of engagement. Conflict means people care. It means they're willing to challenge ideas. It means they're invested in getting this right.

The problem is, most teams confuse conflict with dysfunction. They think disagreement is bad. So they avoid the thing. They stay polite. They nod along. And nothing ever gets solved.

EOS gives you permission to disagree and provides a framework for working through conflict productively. Remember, the goal isn't to make everyone happy. Make the best decision for the business.

Before we move on, let's recap:

- Decision fatigue is real. Exhausting. And killing your meetings.
- IDS gives you a process for making decisions faster and better. Use who-who-one-what. Time-box when you need to. Go around the room to get all voices.
- Rocks create focus and accountability.
- Scorecards give you visibility and truth.
- Check your archive when issues keep coming back.
- Conflict isn't the enemy. Indecision is.

If your meetings feel stuck, it's probably because decisions aren't getting made. The good news? You can fix this. Starting today.

---

[16] The 90-Day World is the EOS concept of operating in quarterly cycles. Ninety days is long enough to accomplish meaningful work and short enough to maintain urgency and accountability. Rocks, quarterly planning, and quarterly conversations all operate within this rhythm. Learn more at EOSWorldwide.com.

"Meetings Suck Less" Realization

Meetings don't fail because people are lazy. They fail because there's no process for making decisions. IDS gives you this process. Use the thing. Every single meeting. And when you're stuck? Remember: you're probably not digging deep enough to find the real issue. Usually, there's a person problem or a structural problem you're dancing around. Name the thing. Solve the thing. Move on.

Up next: Who's running this meeting? And why does it feel like nobody's driving the bus?

3

"WHO THE HELL IS RUNNING THIS MEETING?"

Here's a question you should be able to answer fast: Who's running this meeting?

Not who sent the invite. Not whose calendar the thing lives on. Not who scheduled the room. Who is running this? Who's making the call on what gets discussed, what gets tabled, and when you're done? Who's keeping things on track when someone goes off about their dog's surgery or their big idea for Q3?

If you struggle to answer, your meetings are a mess.

The Three Roles You Should Care About

Back in Chapter 1, we talked about the five deadly sins of meetings. Sin number five was no accountability. And accountability starts with roles.

Every meeting needs three: Owner, Facilitator, and Note Taker.

You need all three. One person doing all three at once is a recipe for dropped balls. The owner is too busy facilitating to think about the objective. The facilitator is scribbling notes while the conversation drifts. Or nobody takes notes because everyone assumes someone else will. We've all been in this meeting. You know how it ends.

The Owner sets the objective. Why are we here? What needs to happen? The Owner invites the right people and makes the meeting worth having in the first place. In a Level 10 Meeting, the Owner is often the Integrator or the team lead who carries the weight of execution during the week.

The Facilitator keeps things moving. Pulls people in. Calls out patterns. Manages the time. Redirects when the group wanders off into the weeds. The Facilitator serves the objective, not their own opinions.

The Facilitator is usually an Integrator or someone in operations. Someone who likes process. Someone who gets excited about checking boxes and solving problems in real time. That person runs the software and owns the agenda. The person who thrives on discipline keeps the train on the tracks.

Most of the time, the Facilitator is not the Visionary. And there's a good reason for this. Visionaries are brilliant at seeing the future, spotting opportunities, and thinking three moves ahead. They're not great at staying in the present. They're emotional. They're inspired by what might be, not what is. And when you're trying to win the week to win the quarter, you need someone anchored in the now.

I've worked with more than 50 clients over 400 session days. When I flip through my mental rolodex of leadership teams, I can count on one hand the number of times the Visionary effectively facilitated their own Level 10 Meeting. Facilitating is not their natural habitat. They want to be in the conversation rather than managing it. They want to think about what's moving, what's next, what's possible. These tasks are exactly what make them great Visionaries. They get to think. They get to participate. They don't have to manage the mechanics of the meeting because someone else is already doing the job.

The Note Taker captures decisions, to-dos, and who owns what. This role gets overlooked, and it shouldn't. Without the Note Taker, everyone leaves with a different version of what happened. Three days later, you get the "wait, what did we decide?" message in Slack. And next week, nobody remembers who agreed to do the thing.

In a great Level 10 Meeting, the Note Taker documents in real time. Everyone sees what's being captured. No mystery. No private notebook nobody else reads. Every decision is there, visible, and agreed upon.

The Note Taker also helps the Facilitator by tracking time. They'll nudge when IDS is running long. They'll flag when the Issues List is getting too packed for one meeting. Think of them as the Facilitator's copilot.

Some teams rotate the Note Taker role. Others keep things consistent. Both work. What doesn't work is having no Note Taker at all. Or having someone scribbling in a journal they take home and never share. Creating a private record helps no one.

For a quick huddle with two or three people, one person covering all three roles gets the job done. But for anything where decisions matter, anything requiring follow-through, you need all three seats filled. Owner. Facilitator. Note Taker.

So before your next meeting, ask: Who owns this meeting? Who's facilitating? Who's taking notes? If you don't have clear answers, you don't have accountability. And without accountability, you're talking, not meeting.

When Meetings Get Hijacked

But here's where things get tricky. Even with clear roles, meetings still get derailed. And guess who's usually the culprit? The Visionary.

I'm not saying this to throw Visionaries under the bus. I love Visionaries. They're the dreamers, the big thinkers, the reason companies grow beyond survival mode. But when they're in a Level 10 Meeting, and everyone else is focused on solving this week's problems, the Visionary is often thinking about next year's vision. It creates tension.

Let me paint you a specific picture from a client session. We were in a Level 10 Meeting, working through the Issues List. The team was IDSing a real customer issue. A sales problem had blown up into a customer retention crisis. This wasn't theoretical. The customer had already told them they were leaving. The team was laser-focused on figuring out the immediate recourse. How do we go back? How do we win the deal back? What's the play?

Then the Visionary stepped in during the solve part. And instead of helping solve the immediate crisis, they started talking about all the future things the company should do to prevent this type of issue. New product features. Long-term customer success strategies. A complete reimagining of the onboarding process.

Were these good ideas? Absolutely. This kind of thinking makes Visionaries invaluable. But helpful right now? Not even a little bit.

The customer was about to walk out the door. Today. You don't win them back with a promise of a better future that doesn't yet exist. Their pain was real and present. The promise of future improvements doesn't make someone say yes when they're already saying goodbye.

And this is the fundamental disconnect. The Visionary sees something the team doesn't see. They're pattern matching across years of experience. They're connecting dots not drawn yet. They're trying to take everyone to a different place, a better place. But mid-crisis is not the right time or place for the conversation.

The room needs to focus on the urgent and important. The Visionary wants to talk about the strategic and visionary. Both matter, but not in the same moment.

The Five Types of Derailment[IP]

Over the years, I've noticed a few patterns in how meetings get hijacked:

The Big Idea Bomb: This is the scenario I just described. The Visionary drops a transformative idea in the middle of solving an immediate problem. The team gets pulled into future-thinking when they need to stay present.

The Tangent Train: Someone mentions a detail reminding another person of something unrelated, and suddenly you're five topics away from where you started. Nobody's steering the conversation back.

The Airtime Hog: One person dominates the conversation with their specific issue. Every week. The meeting becomes their therapy session while everyone else checks their phones.

The Duel: Two strong personalities lock horns on a point not needing this much airtime. The facilitator doesn't intervene, so everyone else waits for the duel to end.

The Premature Solve: Someone jumps to solutions before the team has fully identified and discussed the issue. You end up solving the wrong problem or creating new ones.

All of these patterns have the same root cause: no one is actively facilitating. Or if they are, they're not doing the thing effectively.

When a derailment happens, you feel the room deflate. People shift in their seats. A few glance at each other. Someone checks their phone. The energy drops because everyone's thinking the same thing: "I wish I had the capacity to be in this moment with you. But right now, I've got three people to lay off, a customer to save, and a fire to put out. I can't shift my lens to your view when my present state is on fire."

The cost of a hijacked meeting is wasted focus, momentum, and trust.

The cost of a hijacked meeting is not wasted time. It's wasted focus, wasted momentum, and wasted trust. People start to check out. They stop bringing their A-game because they know the meeting might veer off into future-land at any moment.

Why No One Stops Things

Here's the uncomfortable truth: most people in the room won't stop the derailment. They won't speak up. They won't push back. Why? Because they're afraid.

The meeting hijacker is usually the Visionary or a senior leader—the person with the most authority in the room. And most people aren't willing to risk their job by telling this person to get back on track. They'll go along to get along.

As a Professional EOS Implementer®, I get paid to enter the danger. I call out a derailment because the worst thing to happen would be that I lose a client. The people in the room? They lose their jobs. That is an entirely different calculation.

I've seen this play out over and over. In Quarterly Conversations[17] and Annual Planning Meetings, I'll step in and redirect. "Great idea. Let's capture the thing on the Long-Term Issues List. Right now, we need to solve the immediate problem." And the room exhales. Everyone was thinking it. I said it.

But in a weekly Level 10 Meeting, there's usually no external facil-itator. It's just the team. And if the internal facilitator doesn't have the courage to enter the danger, the meeting stays derailed. The issue doesn't get solved. The team leaves frustrated. And next week, the same thing happens again.

I work with our team at Ninety. And even with all my experience coaching other companies, I still see people hesitate to call out derail-ment. Some folks on our team don't mind calling the meeting a six when everyone else is pretending it's a ten. But there are plenty of people who won't say anything. Not because they're weak. Because entering the danger requires something most workplaces don't naturally cultivate: permission to disagree.

You've got to be in the state of mind where you're thinking, "I'm okay with whatever ramifications happen as a result of my disagreement." It's a tall order when your mortgage depends on this job.

The good news is there is a way to stop derailments without entering the danger. This is why we built the Tangent button into Ninety.

Here's how the thing works. You're in a Level 10 Meeting. Someone raises an issue. You start discussing. Three minutes in, the conversation drifts. Someone brings up a different problem. Someone else jumps on a related topic. Now you're talking about something else entirely.

---

[17]   Quarterly Conversations are informal two-way feedback discussions between a manager and each direct report, held every 90 days. Unlike formal annual reviews, Quarterly Conversations are designed to surface issues early and promote growth in both directions. Learn more at EOSWorldwide.com.

In most meetings, nobody stops this. Everyone sits there thinking, "We're off track," but nobody wants to be the person who says the thing.

With the Tangent button, you don't have to say a word. You press the button. A notification appears on screen. "Tangent flagged." The facilitator sees the alert. The team knows someone thinks we're off track.

No names. No confrontation. No risk.

The facilitator can then say, "Looks like we might be on a tangent. Let's check: are we still solving the original issue, or should we capture this new topic and come back to it?"

The Tangent button removes the personal risk of calling out a derailment. You're not challenging the Visionary. You're not telling your boss they're wrong. You're pressing a button. The software is doing the redirect, not you.

This matters more than you might think.

One of the biggest problems with meeting culture is the invisible hierarchy. The person with the title, the loudest voice, or the longest tenure controls the room. Everyone else self-edits. They hold back. They wait to see what the leader thinks before sharing their perspective.

The Tangent button democratizes the redirect. Anyone in the meeting can utilize it. The intern. The newest team member. The person who usually stays quiet. The button gives them permission to flag the problem without putting themselves in the line of fire.

And here's what happens over time: teams start to trust the process. The first time someone presses the Tangent button, there's tension. "Who pressed the thing?" But after you use the thing a few times, the team gets comfortable. The redirect stops feeling personal. Becomes part of the rhythm.

You're not calling someone out. You're keeping the meeting on track. There's a difference.

I've seen teams go from zero redirects (because nobody wanted to speak up) to three or four Tangent flags per meeting. Not because the meetings got worse. Because the team got braver. The tool gave them permission.

And when you combine the Tangent button with good facilitation, meetings get sharper. You stop the drifts faster. You solve issues instead of discussing them. You build momentum instead of spinning your wheels.

The Tangent button doesn't fix everything. You still need a facilitator willing to act on the feedback. You still need a team committed to healthy conflict. You still need leaders who create psychological safety.

But the tool helps by removing one barrier, making the redirect less personal, and giving people a low-risk way to signal when things are off track.

This is what good software does. It doesn't replace the discipline; it makes the discipline easier to practice.

At Ninety, we use the Tangent button in our own meetings. All the time. Someone flags a tangent. The facilitator checks in. We either redirect or capture the new issue for later. The meeting stays focused. Nobody feels attacked. The process works.

If your team struggles with derailments (and most teams do), give people a tool to flag the thing without entering the danger. Make the redirect anonymous. Remove the personal risk.

You'll be surprised how quickly people start using the thing. And how much better your meetings get when derailments get stopped in real time instead of after the meeting in the parking lot.

The Tangent button isn't magic. It represents permission. Permission to disagree. Permission to redirect. Permission to keep the meeting on track without risking your job.

And permission matters.

The Go-Along-to-Get-Along Trap

When I coach people, it's easy to say, "Hey, don't go along to get along. If you see the thing, say the thing. If you feel the thing, be truthful, specific, and positive." This advice is solid, but executing when you're staring down the Visionary who signs your paycheck is a different game.

This is why facilitation training matters. The facilitator needs to be empowered. Not by title, but by practice and by the team's agreement on the permission to redirect anyone, including the Visionary. Without explicit permission, the facilitator can only go through the motions.

Good teams have a conversation outside the Level 10 Meeting where everyone agrees on the rules. The Visionary says, "If I derail, call me on it. I give you permission." And then (this is critical) when someone does redirect, no one gets defensive. The team honors the interruption and course corrects.

This is difficult, cultural work. But it's the only way to stop the go-along-to-get-along pattern from killing your meetings.

The TSP Framework

So how do you push back without creating conflict? How do you redirect a hijacking without making the Visionary feel shut down?

Use TSP: Truthful, Specific, Positive.

Truthful: "I feel like we're moving away from the immediate problem."

State it as your truth. Not an accusation. Not a judgment. Just how you're experiencing the moment.

Specific: "We were solving how to win this customer back, and now we're talking about long-term product strategy."

Name what's happening. Make the thing concrete. People don't argue with observable facts.

Positive: "I think we should capture those ideas on the Long-Term Issues List and stay focused on solving today's problem. Once we handle this, we revisit the bigger strategy."

Give a path forward. Show you're not dismissing the Visionary's ideas. You're asking for the right time and place to discuss them.

TSP creates space for honesty without triggering defensiveness. Hard to argue with someone who's sharing their truth, being specific, and offering a positive way forward.

The Facilitator's Job

This is why the facilitator role matters so much. A great facilitator isn't reading the agenda and keeping time. They're protecting the room.

They're managing energy. They're making sure the meeting serves a purpose: to solve issues, create clarity, and move the business forward.

A great facilitator knows when to let a conversation breathe and when to cut the thing off. They know when to park an idea and when to dig deeper. They know how to redirect without making people feel dismissed.

Facilitation is a skill. Not something you're born with. Something you develop by practicing, getting feedback, and getting better. Some people are naturals. Most aren't. But everyone improves if they're willing to work on it.

At Ninety, I facilitate our Level 10 Meetings. Some weeks, I do this well. Other weeks, I miss the derailment completely. I'm still learning. Still getting better. It's the job.

When the Facilitator Fails

I once coached a team where the sales manager would constantly hijack the meeting. Every week, he'd flag a problem with one of his deals and make the entire meeting about him. Not in a malicious way. He genuinely thought his issues were the most important things happening in the business. And they were, to him.

But the facilitator saw this happening and didn't have the confidence to shut things down. They kept thinking, "What if people think I don't care about customer issues? What if I come across as dismissive?" So they let things run. Fifteen to twenty minutes of a sixty-minute meeting were consumed by one person's specific deal drama.

And guess what happened? The rest of the team started checking out. They stopped showing up mentally. Some stopped showing up physically. "Sorry, conflict." They'd bail because the meeting had become a waste of their time.

The facilitator's fear of being perceived as uncaring created the exact outcome they were trying to avoid. The team felt like their time didn't matter. Like the meeting wasn't for them. And trust eroded. Week by week, issue by issue, the Level 10 Meeting became something people dreaded instead of something they valued.

Eventually, we had to reset. I pulled the facilitator aside and said, "Your job isn't to make everyone feel heard all the time. Your job is to make sure the meeting accomplishes what it's supposed to accomplish. If someone's issue requires more than five minutes of IDS time, that's a signal the issue needs a different venue. Take the thing offline. Schedule a separate meeting." It's not rude. It's leadership.

The facilitator pushed back. "But won't this person feel shut down?"

"Yes," I said. "But you know what? One person feeling temporarily shut down is better than seven other people feeling permanently ignored."

Took a few weeks, but the facilitator found their footing. They started redirecting. They started protecting the room. They'd say, "This is important and needs more time than we have in this meeting. Let's schedule thirty minutes this afternoon to dig into the thing. For now, let's move to the next issue."

And you know what? The sales manager wasn't offended. He was relieved. Because he needed more than five minutes to solve his complex deal issue. The Level 10 Meeting wasn't the right format. And once he got the dedicated time he needed, he stopped hijacking the weekly meeting.

The team came back to life. People started engaging again. The meeting rating went from sixes and sevens to consistent nines. All because the facilitator learned to protect the room.

Developing Facilitation Skills

Here's the thing about facilitation: it's a skill, not a personality trait. Some people have a natural instinct for it. Most don't. But everyone gets better.

If you're the facilitator and you're struggling, here are a few practical tips I find helpful:

Practice the redirects. Practice saying them out loud.

- "Let's capture this for later."
- "Good point. We table the thing?"
- "We're running long. Let's move on."

The words feel awkward the first dozen times. Then they become natural.

Get feedback. At the end of the meeting, ask the team, "How did I do facilitating today?" Let them be honest. You'll hear things you didn't notice. Someone will say, "You let the IDS on issue three run too long." Or "You didn't pull me in when I had something to say." Feedback is gold.

Watch other facilitators. If you're a Professional EOS Implementer or you work with one, pay attention to how they facilitate. Notice what they say and when they say it. Notice how they manage energy. Steal their best moves.

Own your mistakes. When you miss a derailment or let something run too long, name the thing. "I should have redirected earlier. My bad." The team respects honesty. And this gives you permission to improve.

Remember: facilitation is service. You're not facilitating to look smart or to be in control. You're facilitating to serve the team's ability to solve issues and move forward. When you think of the responsibility as service, the pressure to be perfect drops away.

The Power of Role Clarity

When everyone knows their role, meetings run better. The facilitator facilitates. The Note Taker captures. The team participates. And if someone steps outside their role, it's obvious. The team calls this out and course-corrects.

But when roles are fuzzy, chaos follows. People talk over each other. No one captures action items. Decisions get made but not recorded. And next week, you're having the same conversation again because no one remembers what was decided.

Role clarity is about respect, not control. It honors everyone's time by making sure the meeting does what it's supposed to do.

Winning the Week to Win the Quarter

Role clarity is about respect, not control.

A Level 10 Meeting is supposed to help you win the week, so you win the quarter. Done. You're not solving world hunger. You're not planning the next five years. You're solving the urgent and important issues so you can hit your Rocks and keep the business moving forward.

The Visionary's big ideas might be urgent or important for the next six months or the next year, but not for now. Not today. That's why we have a Long-Term Issues List where ideas go to live until the right moment. During the weekly meeting, the team focuses on what matters now. During Quarterly Conversations, they tackle the bigger, longer-term issues.

This separation keeps everyone sane, prevents the Visionary from feeling like their ideas are being dismissed, and protects the team from drowning in future-thinking when they need to stay present.

Think about this like basketball: if you're trying to win a game and you're down by three points with two minutes left, you don't stop to discuss next season's draft strategy. You focus on the immediate game. You run the plays. You execute. You win or lose based on what you do right now.

The Level 10 Meeting is your two-minute drill. The Quarterly is your off-season planning. Both matter. But they serve different purposes. And confusing them kills your ability to do either one well.

What Good Facilitation Looks Like

I've been in hundreds of Level 10 Meetings over the years. The best ones have a few things in common:

The facilitator starts on time. Not five minutes late. Not "Let's wait for Bob." On time. Because when you wait for late people, you're teaching everyone the start time doesn't matter. And if the start time doesn't matter, nothing matters.

The agenda is clear and visible. Everyone knows what's coming and what's expected. The agenda isn't a surprise. The same every week. Segue.[18] Scorecard. Rock Review. Customer/Employee Headlines. To-Do List. IDS. Conclude. This structure creates predictability. And predictability creates space for real work.

The facilitator protects the IDS process. This is where most meetings fall apart. When someone starts solving before they've fully discussed the issue, the facilitator redirects. When someone tries to identify a new issue in the middle of solving the current one, the facilitator captures the thing on the Issues List for later. The facilitator guards the boundaries of each step.

The facilitator manages energy. They notice when someone's checked out and pull them back in. "Sarah, you've been quiet. What's your take?" They notice when the room is stuck in analysis paralysis and push for a decision. "We've been discussing this for ten minutes. Let's vote and move forward." They read the room and adjust accordingly.

The facilitator ends on time. Because if you don't respect the hour, you won't respect the process. And if you regularly run over, people will start scheduling things right after the meeting to force the thing to end. That's a sure symptom of broken facilitation.

But here's what great facilitation looks like in action: invisible. When a meeting flows well, you don't notice the facilitator working. You notice things keep moving. Issues get solved. Decisions get made. Everyone leaves with clarity.

The facilitator is like a good sports referee. You don't want to notice them. But when they're not doing their job, the whole game falls apart.

---

[18]   The Segue is the five-minute opening of a Level 10 Meeting where each team member shares a personal and professional best from the past week. The Segue transitions the team from working "in" the business to working "on" the business. Learn more at EOSWorldwide.com/Blog/The-Level-10-Meeting."

The Facilitator's Energy Management Toolkit

Let me give you some practical moves great facilitators use:

The Redirect: "Great point. Let's capture this on the Issues List and come back to the thing after we finish this one."

The Time Check: "We've got three more issues to discuss and fifteen minutes left. Let's keep moving."

The Pull-In: "I notice a few people haven't weighed in yet. What are we missing?"

The Decision Push: "I'm hearing a lot of discussion but no clear path forward. Let's IDS this: What's the issue we're trying to solve?"

The Parking Lot: "This feels like needing more time than we have. Let's move the issue to our Long Term Issues list and address it at the Quarterly, and keep moving."

The Pattern Call-Out: "This is the third week we've discussed this without solving the thing. What's blocking us from making a decision?"

These aren't scripts. They're tools. And the best facilitators develop their own language over time. But they all do the same thing: they keep the meeting moving forward.

A Final Thought on Derailment

Derailment isn't always bad. Sometimes the Visionary sees something the team doesn't. Sometimes the big idea is exactly what the business needs. Sometimes the derailment is a gift.

But even gifts need the right wrapping. Even great ideas need the right context. And even brilliant Visionaries need a facilitator who says, "I love where you're going. Let's park this for the right conversation."

Because meetings aren't about who has the best ideas. They're about solving problems, making decisions, and moving forward. And you can't do this if no one's running the show.

"Meetings Suck Less" Realization

Meetings don't fail because people aren't smart enough. They fail because no one's running them. Role clarity (especially knowing who facilitates) transforms chaos into progress. When everyone knows their job, the meeting does the job. And when the meeting does the job, work gets lighter.

Next up: We're going to talk about fake productivity. You know, those "alignment sessions" and "quick syncs" that make you feel busy without accomplishing anything. Time to call this out.

4

STOP SYNCING AND START SOLVING

You know what kills companies faster than bad strategy? Accomplishing nothing.

I'm not talking about the occasional dud. Every team has those. I'm talking about the recurring, calendar-clogging, soul-draining meetings existing for no other reason than... they exist. The daily stand-up that has been going on for three years. The "quick sync" that never ends. The "alignment session" where nobody gets aligned.

These meetings are productivity theater. They look like work. They feel like work. But they're not work. They're expensive ways to avoid work.

Walk into most companies and check their calendars. You'll find meeting after meeting after meeting. Status updates are just glorified Slack messages. A "touch base" never touches anything. "Syncs" leave everyone more out of sync than before. And when you ask people what gets decided in these meetings, they give you the blank stare.

Nothing gets decided. Nothing gets solved. The same issues show up next week. And the week after. And the week after.

This isn't a meeting problem. This is a discipline problem, and it's costing you more than you think.

When Check-Ins Stop Being Useful

Here's something I see all the time: a team starts a daily stand-up because they've got a real problem. Production's behind. Clients are angry. The warehouse is a mess. So they huddle up every morning for fifteen minutes to get everyone on the same page, and boom. Problems start getting solved.

Fast forward six months. The problem's gone. Production's smooth. Clients are happy. But guess what's still happening? The daily stand-up. Same time. Same people. Same fifteen minutes.

Except now nobody's solving anything. They're connecting. Chatting. Getting their social fix. And look, I'm not against people connecting. Connection matters. Trust requires connection. But when your "production meeting" turns into a coffee klatch, you've got a problem.

The meeting lost purpose.

In EOS, we don't prescribe daily stand-ups in the framework. It often surprises people, especially because other systems love them. Scaling Up swears by them. Cameron Herold wrote a whole book about them. And hey, if they're solving a specific problem, like coordinating a shop floor, refreshing everyone on the day's numbers, or closing out the day for tomorrow, great. Productive.

A fifteen-minute stand-up on the production floor makes total sense when you need to assign today's work, check yesterday's numbers, and make sure everyone knows which machine is down. Focused. Purposeful. "Coming in hot" for the day.

But where things go sideways is when the critical problem gets solved, but the meeting sticks around because it's now habit. Nobody questions the thing. It becomes part of the culture. "We always meet at 8 a.m." Okay, but why? "Because we always have."

That answer is an obituary for productivity.

We had some of this happen at Ninety, too. COVID hit, and suddenly we needed more frequent check-ins. The velocity changed. The volume changed. Remote work created new challenges. So we added meetings to help people stay connected, stay informed, stay sane.

Made total sense at the time.

But then the crisis passed. Work normalized. Systems improved. And some of those meetings? They stuck around. Not because they were solving problems. Because people liked them. They got to see each other. They got emotional satisfaction from the connection.

You have to make a choice as a leader: are we running a business or a social club?

The Real Question: What Are We Solving For?

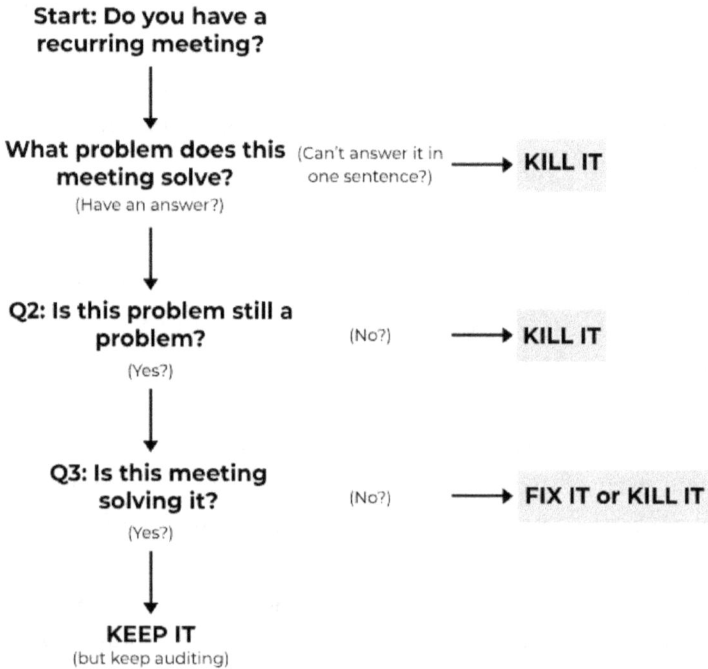

Remember those three questions we asked when we performed the Calendar Audit? Those are the real questions that you should be able to answer about every meeting.

- What problem does this meeting solve?
- Is this problem still a problem?
- Is this meeting solving the problem?

If your answer to the first is "Well, I don't know. We always meet on Tuesdays at 10," congratulations. You described a ritual, not a meeting. And rituals are great for holidays and weddings. They're terrible for running a business.

The "Got a Sec?" Trap

Let me tell you about my least favorite meeting: the drive-by.

You're in the zone. Deep work. Making progress. Then someone walks by (physically or virtually) and says, "Hey, got a sec?"

No. I don't. Because they don't mean "a sec." They mean thirty minutes. An hour. And whatever I was doing? Dead. The flow state's gone. The momentum's toast. And usually, whatever they wanted to talk about could have waited.

This is where EOS discipline saves your life. If you've got a weekly Level 10 Meeting scheduled (every Tuesday at 9 a.m., same time, same people), you say, "Does this need to happen right now, or do we add the thing to the Issues List for Tuesday?"

Nine times out of ten, things can wait. And when things wait, you protect your time. You protect their time. And you keep the team focused on what matters.

The L10™ creates boundaries. It gives you permission to defer and trains your team to think before they interrupt. Is this urgent and important, or is this loud?

Most things feel urgent until you give them 72 hours. Then they're either solved or irrelevant.

When Meetings Turn Into Firefights

Now, let's be real. Sometimes the business is on fire, and I have had clients say dumpster fire: production problems, client emergencies, supply chain nightmares, software launches gone sideways, etc. In those moments, waiting for Tuesday doesn't cut it.

The theory behind the weekly meeting in EOS is simple: anything that can wait should wait. But if you're in a firefight and waiting four days might sink you, you adjust. The velocity's too high. The volume's too intense. The change is too fast. You need more touch points to keep the wheels from coming off.

So you add frequency. Not every day, but Monday, Wednesday, and Friday. Or you add a check-in at the beginning, middle, and end of the week. And you focus on the thing: "What's the most urgent and important thing keeping us from success tomorrow? What do we solve today so we don't burn down tomorrow?"

The mentality should stay short, focused, and positive.

But here's the catch: you've got to keep people disciplined on what goes into the meeting.

Because what happens (and I've seen this dozens of times) is people start treating the daily check-in like a dumping ground. They put everything on the short-term Issues List: problems that can absolutely wait until Monday's L10, topics that aren't urgent at all, and strategic questions needing more than 15 minutes of thought.

Suddenly, your fifteen-minute production check-in turns into a forty-five-minute rabbit hole where you're debating marketing strategy or arguing about whether to hire another account executive, which was never the meeting's purpose.

You've got to coach the team. "Hey, this isn't what this meeting's for. It goes on the long-term Issues List. We'll IDS it Monday. Right now, we're focused on what breaks if we don't solve the thing in the next 24 hours."

Compartmentalization of short-term issues versus long-term issues takes practice. Weekly cadence versus daily cadence. Urgent versus important. Beyond the quarter versus this quarter versus this week versus today.

Most teams aren't used to thinking this way. They're used to throwing everything into one big pile and hoping someone sorts things out. But once they get the discipline, everything speeds up. Because now you're solving the right problems at the right time in the right meetings.

And clarity? That's what makes work flow.

The Social-Emotional Meeting Trap

Some meetings stick around because they meet an emotional need, not a business need.

People feel disconnected, especially in remote or hybrid environments. They miss the casual conversations. The hallway chats. The quick problem-solving happening when you bump into someone at the coffee maker. So they schedule meetings to recreate this. To see each other. To chat. To feel like part of something.

Seeking social interaction is totally human. Connection is one of the core elements of trust. But don't pretend this is a business meeting when this is a social hour.

If your team needs connection (and they do; everyone does), provide it intentionally. Build it in and name it: "This is our connection time. This is where we talk about life, hobbies, families, whatever. This isn't about solving business problems."

But don't let connection hijack your tactical meetings. Because when you over-schedule yourself with socializing meetings disguised as productivity, you rob people of genuine connection. You turn what should be authentic into performative. And you waste the time you've set aside to solve problems.

Don't let connection hijack your tactical meetings.

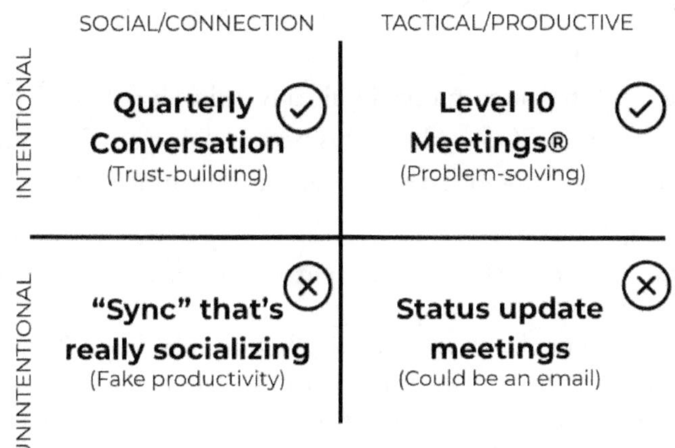

Connection has three elements I always talk about with clients: frequency (how often we see each other), duration (how long we spend together), and depth (how deep we go beyond sports, news, and weather).

If you don't give people some of this (if you don't create space for frequency, duration, and depth), trust starts to wane. People feel like cogs. Like numbers. Like they don't matter.

And when trust wanes, everything else breaks. Communication suffers. Collaboration dies. People start leaving.

So yes, absolutely create connection time. Don't disguise the thing as something else. And don't let connection time bleed into the meetings where you need to get work done.

The L10 is for solving problems. The Quarterly Conversation is for building trust. Both matter. But they're different meetings with different purposes.

The Quarterly Conversation: A Trust-Based Meeting

In EOS, we've got a meeting specifically designed for connection: the Quarterly Conversation.[19]

No agenda. No scorecard. No Issues List. No Rocks review. You and your direct report, once a quarter, going off-site. Grab coffee, take a walk, sit somewhere besides the office. And check in.

"How are you doing? What's on your mind? What do you need from me?"

As the leader, you're probably already thinking about The People Analyzer® tool from EOS.[20] How's this person doing on Core Values? Do they Get It, Want It, and have the Capacity to do it (GWC®)?[21] Those

---

[19]   To access the complete Quarterly Conversation tool, visit EOSWorldwide.com/Quarterly-Conversations.

[20]   You can download the People Analyzer at EOSWorldwide.com/People.

[21]   GWC stands for Gets it, Wants it, and has the Capacity to do it. GWC is the EOS tool for evaluating whether a person is the right fit for a given seat on the Accountability Chart. Learn more at EOSWorldwide.com.

assessments are important. But in this meeting, you're not there to deliver a verdict. You're not there to lecture or evaluate.

You're there to ask. To listen. To be curious.

This is a "how" question, not a "what" question. You're not asking, "What did you accomplish?" You're asking, "How are you feeling about the work? How are you managing the load? How can I help you be more successful?"

And here's the thing: the Quarterly Conversation rebuilds trust. You're giving people space to share work challenges, personal stuff, frustrations they haven't voiced, and ideas they've been sitting on. Whatever's real.

Sometimes, a problem for the Issues List comes up. Great. Add it. But don't make that the point of the meeting. The point is: I see you. You matter. Let's connect.

The Quarterly Conversation serves a different purpose from your L10. Both are critical. The L10 is where you solve problems. The Quarterly Conversation is where you build trust, making problem-solving possible.

What About One-on-Ones?

People ask me about one-on-ones all the time. "Kris, should I meet with my direct reports every week? Every two weeks? Monthly?"

And my answer frustrates them: it depends on the person.

Look, I love Kolbe. I love Myers-Briggs. I love DISC, StrengthsFinder, and any tool helping me understand the human on the other side. Because here's the deal: people are different. And what works for one person doesn't work for another.

Some people (especially "Feelers" on Myers-Briggs) need weekly one-on-ones. They need regular check-ins to feel connected, supported, and heard. If you're only meeting with them quarterly, they feel abandoned. They start to think you don't care.

Other people (more "Thinker" types) might be perfectly fine with quarterly check-ins. They don't need the constant touch points. In fact, too many meetings feel suffocating to them. They'd rather get their work done and loop you in when needed.

Neither approach is wrong, just different.

So here's what I coach leaders to do: Ask your people, "What works for you? How often do you need to connect with me? What helps you do your best work?"

And then honor the commitment. Even if it's different from what you need. Even if it means you're meeting with one person weekly and another person monthly.

Customization isn't weakness. It's leadership. Because when you give people what they need (not what your calendar prefers or what some management book prescribed), they show up better. They trust you more. And the work gets done faster.

Customization isn't weakness. It's leadership.

The "Rate Your Meeting" Breakthrough

Alright, let's talk about the tool changing everything: the meeting rating.

At the end of every meeting (and I mean every meeting, not the important ones), ask everyone to rate the experience on a scale of 1 to 10. No hiding. No fudging. Everyone shares their number.

Ten isn't perfection. Ten is high performance. You're aiming for consistent 8s, 9s, and 10s. Anything below an 8 means something's broken.

Here's why this works: accountability.

When you know your meeting's getting rated, you show up differently. As the meeting leader, you prep. You create a real agenda. You stay on topic. You don't let Bob hijack the conversation with his side issue about the parking lot policy. And if the conversation starts to drift, someone in the room will call things out because they know they're about to give this meeting a 5.

One thing I've seen consistently is this: when teams first start using EOS and rating their meetings, they usually land in the 7s and 8s. Fine. Typical. They're learning. They're getting the muscle memory.

But as they get better at Level 10 Meetings (as they learn to IDS Issues effectively, as they stop tolerating drift, as they hold each other accountable), those ratings climb. Six months in, teams are consistently hitting 8s and 9s. A year in, 9s and 10s become normal.

And when ratings climb, everything else improves. Morale goes up. Productivity increases. People start looking forward to meetings instead of dreading them.

I've never met anyone who said, "Man, I loved leaving this meeting confused about what we decided." But I've met hundreds of people who've told me, "This L10 was the most productive hour of my week."

The difference? Discipline. Structure. And a rating system to force honesty.

How the Rating System Works

When you're first rolling out meeting ratings, people get nervous. "What if I give this a low score? Will my boss get mad?"

You've got to set the tone: low scores are data, not insults.

If someone rates the meeting a 5, they are providing valuable feedback. Don't get defensive. Ask, "What made this a 5 for you? What would make this an 8 next time?"

Sometimes the answer's obvious. "We didn't have an agenda." "We spent thirty minutes talking in circles about the same issue." "Three people were on their phones the whole time." "We ran twenty minutes over, and I missed my next meeting."

Great. Now you know what to fix.

Sometimes the answer is deeper. "I didn't feel heard." "My issue never made the Issues List." "I'm still confused about who owns this decision."

Even better. Now you're uncovering problems you didn't even know existed.

The rating isn't the point. The conversation after the rating is the point.

And here's what happens over time: people get more honest. The first few ratings are usually inflated. Everyone gives 8s because they don't want to rock the boat. But once they see low scores lead to improvements (not punishment), they start telling the truth.

The Cost of Bad Meetings

Let's do some quick math that will make your CFO cry.

Say you've got ten people in a meeting. Let's say the average salary across the team is $75,000 a year, which works out to about $36 an hour per person. Multiply by ten people, and you're spending $360 for every hour those people sit in a room together.

Now add up how many meetings you've got each week. Leadership meeting. Department meetings. Project updates. Status syncs. One-on-ones. Let's be conservative and say you've got 20 hours of meetings a week involving those 10 people. $7,200 a week. Multiply by 52 weeks, and you're looking at $374,400 a year.

Almost $400,000. On meetings.

Now ask yourself: how many of those meetings moved the business forward? How many resulted in clear decisions? How many solved problems?

If you're honest, probably less than half.

Which means you're burning $200,000 a year on meetings, yet accomplishing nothing. We're not even counting the opportunity cost. The deals are not closing because your sales team is stuck in "alignment sessions." The projects are not launching because your engineers are trapped in status updates. The momentum is dying while everyone's debating whether to use blue or green for the logo.

Bad meetings don't waste time. They waste money. They waste talent. They waste opportunity.

And here's the killer: most companies have no idea how much they're hemorrhaging.

I worked with a manufacturing client a few years back who complained about low output. They had enough people. The systems were solid. But somehow, production kept falling short. So we audited their meetings.

Turns out, the leadership team was pulling line supervisors into meetings fifteen to twenty hours a week. Strategy sessions. Planning meetings. Updates that should have been emails. And while those supervisors sat in conference rooms, their teams floundered. Problems went unsolved. Decisions got delayed. Production stalled.

We cut the meeting load in half. Focused only on the meetings that solved problems. And guess what? Production jumped 30 percent in two months.

Same people. Same systems. Fewer meetings.

Meetings aren't free. They're one of your biggest expenses. Treat them like the investment they are.

Practical Exercises: Fix One Meeting This Week

You don't have to overhaul your entire meeting culture today. You'll be overwhelmed and quit before you start. Pick one meeting—one bad one that everyone dreads—and use the Five-Step Fix.

Here's what to do:

Step 1: Define the problem this meeting solves. Write the thing down. One sentence. "This meeting exists to [solve X problem]."

Can't keep it to one sentence? The meeting probably doesn't have a real purpose.

Step 2: Ask the team the hard questions. "Is this problem still a problem? And if so, is this meeting solving the thing?"

If the answer's no, kill the meeting. Seriously. Cancel the thing. See what breaks. (Spoiler: probably nothing.)

If the answer's yes, move to step 3.

Step 3: Clean things up. Add structure. Create an agenda (not a list of topics, but a framework). For an L10, that structure is Segue, Scorecard, Rock Review, Headlines, To-Do Review, IDS, and Conclude.

Build an Issues List. Teach the team how to add to it before the meeting, not during.

Practice IDS. Identify the real issue. Discuss the thing until everyone's clear. Solve with a concrete decision and to-dos.

Step 4: Rate the thing. At the end, everyone shares their number. 1 to 10. No hiding. And then ask, "What would make this an 8 or higher next time?"

Write down what people say. And improve on those points next time.

Step 5: Rinse and repeat next week. This isn't a one-time thing. Make it a discipline. Keep rating. Keep improving. Keep asking if the meeting's still solving the problem it was designed to solve.

One meeting at a time is all you need.

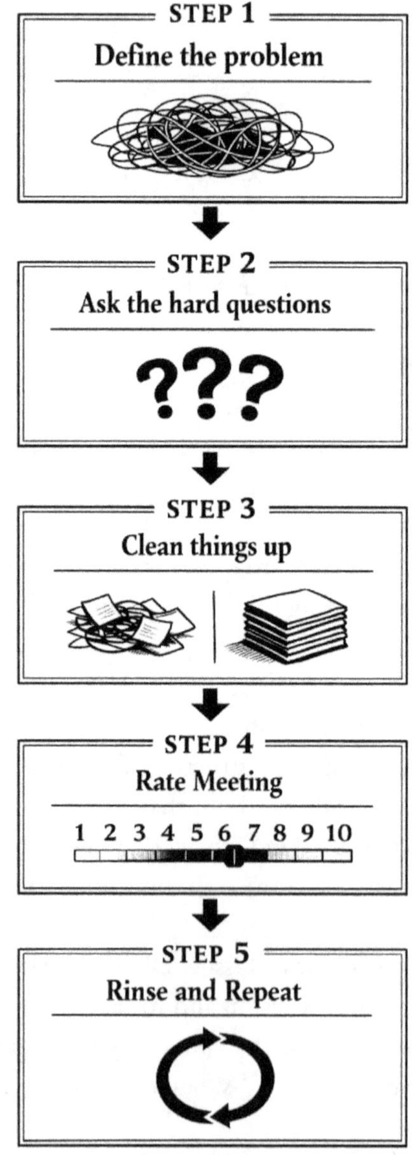

The Shift: From Fake Work to Real Work

Here's what I want you to take away from this chapter: Meetings are not the enemy. Bad meetings are the enemy.

When meetings are disciplined, focused, and purposeful, they're your strongest tool. They're where alignment happens. Where decisions get made. Where teams build trust and solve problems together.

But when meetings become theater (when they're something you do because it's Tuesday and the meeting is on the calendar), they rot your company from the inside.

The good news? You can fix this. Right now. Today.

Start small. Pick one meeting. Apply the tools in this chapter. Rate it. Improve it. Repeat.

And when one meeting starts working, pick another. And another. Build the discipline. Train the muscle. Make it normal for your team to demand more from every meeting they attend.

Your time matters. Your team's time matters. And every hour you waste in a useless meeting is an hour you could have spent building something important.

Stop syncing. Start solving.

"Meetings Suck Less" Realization

Meetings don't suck because people suck. Meetings suck because they've lost their purpose. Reconnect every meeting to problem-solving. Rate the results. Fix what's broken. And watch your team go from meeting-fatigued to meeting-focused.

RED FLAGS CHECKLIST:
IS YOUR MEETING **FAKE PRODUCTIVITY?**

- [ ] We've been doing this meeting for years, and nobody remembers why it was started.
- [ ] No one preps for the thing.
- [ ] The same topics come up every time without getting solved.
- [ ] People check their phones or multitask during the thing.
- [ ] When this ends, nobody knows what was decided.
- [ ] Someone always says, "Let's circle back on this".
- [ ] You leave feeling more confused than when you walked in.
- [ ] If you canceled the thing, nothing would break.

3+ checked? Time to **KILL** the meeting.

Up next: Let's talk about what happens when the fearless leader shows up. (Spoiler: Everyone shuts down. And this is a you problem.)

5

THE VISIONARY'S CURSE: YOU SHOWED UP AND EVERYONE SHUT DOWN

Monday morning. I walk into an annual planning meeting with a leadership team I've been working with for a while. Six people sit around the table. Three of them are brand new to the team. We're in day one of a two-day session. The energy in the room feels tentative—new people size up the old guard while the old guard wonders how these new folks are going to change the dynamic.

Before I get my laptop open, the Visionary stands up.

"Look, I know I dominate meetings," he says.

The room goes quiet. You hear a pin drop. A couple people shift in their chairs. Someone takes a sudden interest in their coffee.

"I try hard not to. I want you guys to enter the danger and have healthy conflict. That's why Kris is here. To make sure I say less and listen more."

He looks around the room. Makes eye contact with each person. Then he turns to me.

"He's gonna make sure I'm opening those doors for you to walk through and keep us on track to do things healthy for us. But I need you guys to weigh in."

Pretty awesome, right?

I've been coaching this team for a while. We hit a ceiling about a year ago. They moved away from the EOS framework for a bit and tried to do things on their own. Things got messy. So the Visionary called me back in.

The fact he's starting the annual this way tells me he gets things now. He understands how his presence (his voice, his opinions, his energy) either opens the room or shuts the thing down. And he's choosing to open the thing.

Fast forward to the next day. I'm in New York for a quarterly with a different client. $100 million company. Another dominant Visionary who built the business over fourteen years. They've hit a ceiling, and they're trying to figure out their stuff.

Different industry. Different team. Different Visionary. Same exact issue.

He started the meeting the same way: "Here's the problem. Given the opportunity, I will tell you all what to do today."

He let things hang in the air for a second.

"I know that's not how we scale. So I need you guys to lean in. Kris is gonna facilitate and make sure everyone gets space. We've got some introverts here. You need to share your perspectives and your opinions."

Then he did something interesting. He took out a notebook and moved his chair back from the table about six inches, creating physical space to match the mental space he's trying to create.

Your presence changes everything.

Two Visionaries. Two days. Two different cities. Same exact playbook.

Why? Because they've learned something most leaders take years to figure out: your presence changes everything.

These weren't their first rodeos. Both had been through the pain of watching their teams shut down when they walked in the room. Both had gotten feedback (probably painful feedback) about how their leadership style was creating bottlenecks. Both had done enough self-reflection to know they needed help managing their own impact.

Here's the thing about Visionary dynamics. The curse isn't being too present. The problem is being present without realizing how present you are. You think you're participating, but your team knows you're doing way more than participating.

"I know I dominate meetings. Kris will help."

The Seagull Problem

We call it the Seagull Problem. You know the type. They fly in, dump on everything, and fly out.

They are late to the meeting. Ill-informed. On their phone the whole time. Leave early because of "more urgent issues."

And the team? They spend the rest of the week cleaning up the mess.

I see this all the time. The Visionary shows up fifteen minutes late to the Level 10 Meeting. Hasn't looked at the Scorecard. Hasn't updated their Rocks. The team's been waiting, wondering if they should start without this person.

Then the Visionary walks in, jumps straight to their pet issue, derails the agenda, makes three decisions contradicting what the team decided last week, and leaves early for a "critical customer call."

The team sits there after the Visionary leaves. Someone finally says, "So... are we still doing what we agreed on last week, or...?"

Nobody knows. Because the seagull flew through.

This isn't bad leadership; it's meeting sabotage. You're not present enough to help, but you're present enough to hurt. And your team knows this.

Here's what you're not seeing while you're half-checked out on your phone: people stop talking. They stop contributing. They start looking at each other with this "should I say something?" glance. The air goes out of the room.

When you finally look up from your email and ask, "Any questions?" they all shake their heads no. Not because they don't have questions. Because they've learned that asking them doesn't help.

I worked with a Visionary once who would come into the weekly leadership meeting, interrupt whoever was talking, announce some new idea he'd had over the weekend, assign the thing to people on the spot, then check out mentally for the rest of the hour. Week after week. Same pattern.

His team learned to nod and smile. They'd hold the real meeting after he left. They called it "the meeting after the meeting." Sound familiar?

This Visionary couldn't figure out why execution was so slow. Why people weren't bought in. Why the team seemed disengaged.

I'll tell you why: because he trained them to be disengaged. Every time he showed up late, unprepared, distracted, or left early, he sent a message. The message was: "This meeting doesn't matter. You don't matter. I've got more important things to do."

And guess what? His team internalized the message.

The Power You Don't See

There's this thing called psychological power distortion. Big fancy term for a simple truth: your title creates gravity.

When you walk into the room, you change the temperature. People calibrate their honesty based on your mood. They edit their ideas based on what they think you want to hear. And if you're not careful, you end up surrounded by people who only tell you what you want to know.

I watched this play out in the New York quarterly. We got to an issue about a former Chief Revenue Officer. Best friend of the Visionary. The guy had been demoted twice. First from CRO to sales leader. Then to individual contributor. Now, he didn't report to anybody because he refused to report to anyone.

Think about this for a second. In a company with 350 people, there's one person who doesn't report to anyone. By choice. Because he said no.

But he's on a couple key accounts. And nobody knows how to handle things.

The new sales leaders (the ones trying to run the sales organization) are looking at each other during this discussion like, "What the hell are we supposed to do? He blows off meetings. Doesn't respond to us. Won't give us visibility into his accounts. We have no idea what's happening with those customers."

As I'm facilitating this, I'm thinking: someone needs to go tell this guy he's out. It's not complicated. You don't have someone who refuses to be part of the organization still be part of the organization.

But they're all frozen. I see this in their body language. The head of sales is looking down at his notes. The head of HR is doing the thing where she's nodding, but her eyes are saying, "This is a disaster." The CFO is stone-faced, jaw clenched.

And I'm sitting there wondering: do they not see the issue? Or are they afraid to name the thing for what it is?

I didn't know he was the Visionary's best friend yet. But they all know. And this knowledge is paralyzing them.

This is what power distortion looks like. A problem that would take five minutes to solve in any other context becomes a weeks-long (months-long?) nightmare because of a relationship at the top.

The issue isn't complicated. The issue is: nobody wants to be the one to tell the Visionary his best friend has to go.

So they've been creating workarounds. Having side conversations. Protecting the Visionary from having to face the thing. And in the process, they've created a situation where the entire sales organization is being held hostage by one person's refusal to participate in the structure.

We're working through the issue using IDS. I'm going around the room, making space for everybody. Getting each person's perspective.

What's the real issue here? What's this costing us? What's the impact on the organization?

People are dancing around things at first. Talking about "communication challenges," "alignment issues," and "unclear reporting structure." All true. None of it touches the heart of the matter.

I get to Jake, the CTO. He's been mostly quiet up until this point. But I see him processing. He's one of those people who doesn't speak until he has something worth saying.

He looks directly at the Visionary.

"Hey, man. I know he's a close friend. But the pain he's causing us is disrespecting this team. You gotta do something."

There it is. The issue.

The room shifts. You feel it. Everyone sits up a little straighter. A couple of people nod. Someone exhales like they've been holding their breath.

Jake said what everyone was thinking. But more importantly, he said the thing directly to the Visionary. Not to me. Not to the team. To the person who needed to hear it.

And you know what the Visionary did? He didn't get defensive. He didn't make excuses. He didn't try to explain away the behavior. He apologized. To the whole room.

"I'm sorry. You're right. I need to own this."

Right there? Leadership. A Visionary who's secure enough to be called out and mature enough to own the thing.

Then he got empathetic, which is also right: "I know his wife, I know his kids. I'm concerned about what happens to him."

And here's where things get good. The team pushed back. Hard. Because they finally felt safe enough to tell the truth.

The Head of Sales said, "This is not on us. This company does not provide jobs for people who don't want them. We gave him a job; he doesn't want it. Clearly. He decided to do something different. We gotta take action."

The Head of HR added, "And every day we let this continue, we send a message to everyone else. We're saying the rules don't apply equally. We're saying relationships matter more than performance."

Another leader spoke up: "We've given him chances. Multiple chances. He's been demoted twice. We've tried to find places where he was successful. But at some point, we have to acknowledge he's chosen not to be part of the team."

When I stepped in, I said, "The beauty of the toolset is it's not on you personally. You created a seat. He doesn't want the thing. He doesn't regard the reporting and support lines you've created. So today's the last day."

The Visionary tried one more time. "What if we give him six months? We'll work with him. He—"

"No. We have to be done. This is so dysfunctional. And we get rated as leaders by the actions we don't take as much as the actions we do take."

Boom. Truth bomb.

She's absolutely right. Your team is watching. When you don't take action on the obvious stuff, they don't forget. Because while you're protecting your friend, the rest of the team's in pain.

They're covering for him. They're losing deals because he's not responsive. They're getting questions from customers they can't answer because he won't share information. They're watching you choose his comfort over their ability to do their jobs.

And with every day passing, they trust you a little less.

The Visionary sat there for a minute. You see him processing. Wrestling with things. This is his friend. His actual friend. Not a colleague or someone he hired. Someone who's been to his house. Someone who knows his family.

But he's also a Visionary. And he's got 350 people counting on him to make good decisions. And sometimes good decisions hurt.

He looked around the room. "You're right. I've been avoiding this. I need to handle this."

Then he set a timeline. Not "someday" or "eventually." A real timeline. They agreed he'd have the conversation this week. They agreed on severance terms. They agreed on how to message things to the team and to the customers.

The whole thing took twenty minutes once they finally got to the real issue. Twenty minutes to solve a problem festering for months.

Why did things take so long? Because nobody felt safe enough to name the thing. Until Jake did. And once he did, everyone else did too.

This kind of breakthrough can happen when you have the right people in the room, the right process to work through issues, and a leader who's willing to hear hard truths.

Why This Is So Hard

Let me tell you why situations like this are so common. Founders build companies with people they know. Friends. Family. Former colleagues. People they trust. People who were there in the early days when nobody else believed in the vision.

These relationships are real. They matter. They're part of why the company exists in the first place.

But here's the problem: the skills it takes to get you to $1 million are not the same skills that will get you to $10 million. And those skills are definitely not the skills you need to reach $100 million.

As the company scales, roles change. Expectations change. What used to work stops working. And sometimes the people who were perfect for the early stage aren't the right people for the next stage. Don't view it as failure. It's growth.

But when the person who isn't the right fit anymore is your best friend? Now you've got a problem. Because you're not evaluating performance. You're weighing performance against a relationship. Against history. Against loyalty. Against all the times they showed up when nobody else would. And the math is impossible.

So most leaders do what the Visionary did: they avoid things. They hope things will get better. They create workarounds. They protect the person. They protect themselves from having to make the hard call.

And in doing so, they hurt everyone else.

The team knows. They always know. They see the special treatment. They see the lack of accountability. They see the double standard. And they make a choice: either call things out and risk the relationship with the Visionary, or stay quiet and let the dysfunction continue.

Most people stay quiet. Jake didn't. And his boldness broke things open.

How to Set the Table

Look, if you're a Visionary, CEO, or anyone with a big title, your team needs you. But they don't need you to solve everything. They need you to create space for them to solve things.

Both those Visionaries I mentioned at the start of this chapter? They didn't walk into the room hoping things would be different. They intentionally set the table. They created conditions for good things to happen.

Here are the 5 Steps to Setting the Table that they used:

1. Name the Power Dynamic Out Loud

Don't pretend the thing doesn't exist. Acknowledge what's going on. "I know I dominate meetings. Given the opportunity, I will tell you all what to do."

The second you name the thing, you take some of the power away.

I've watched this work in dozens of sessions. The Visionary stands up at the beginning of an annual and says, "Look, I know people stop talking when I talk. I know the weight of my opinion shuts down other perspectives. So today, I'm asking you to push back on me. Challenge my assumptions. If you disagree, say so."

You'll feel awkward the first time you do this. Do it anyway.

Your team already knows you have power. They're already calibrating everything they say based on what they think you want to hear. By acknowledging it, you give them permission to stop calibrating.

2. Tell Them What You're NOT There to Do

This is the script you need: "I'm not here to make every decision. I'm here to help you make better decisions."

Give them permission to push back. To challenge. To disagree. Say this explicitly. They won't believe you until you prove it's true.

In one of my recent quarterlies with a client, the Visionary said things clearly: "I'm not here to tell you what to do. I'm here to make sure we're solving the right problems." Then he followed through. When people brought up issues, he asked questions instead of giving answers.

"What do you think we should do?" "What have you already tried?" "What's blocking you from moving forward?"

Notice what he's not saying? He's not saying "Here's what I think we should do" or "Why haven't you done this already?" He's creating space for them to think.

That is the difference between a leader who empowers and a leader who dominates.

3. Bring in a Facilitator

Did you notice how both those Visionaries brought me in to run the meeting? Smart. You don't facilitate and participate at the same level. Pick one.

If you're the one with all the power in the room, you need someone else holding the structure. Someone who will cut you off when you're talking too much. Someone who will call on the quiet person in the corner.

A good facilitator will protect the process from you. When you start going down a rabbit hole, they redirect. When you try to solve the issue before the team has had a chance to discuss the thing, they slow you down. When you're about to make a decision that should be coming from the team, they step in.

You might be thinking, "I don't need someone to facilitate my meetings. I'm perfectly capable of running them myself."

You're probably right. You're also probably the problem.

If you have significant power in the organization, you need an external facilitator. Period. Your team will never fully engage if you're both playing the game and reffing the thing.

4. Listen More Than You Talk

I know. You built the company. You have the vision. You've been thinking about this problem for six months, while they heard about it only ten minutes ago. It doesn't mean you get to talk the whole time.

In a 90-minute meeting, you should be talking for twenty minutes. Max. The rest of the time? Listen. Ask questions. Let the team work the issue.

I track this sometimes in sessions. I'll count how much time each person speaks. And you know what happens? The Visionary is usually shocked when they see the data.

"I talked for twenty minutes? Felt like I barely said anything!"

Exactly. Good facilitation should feel like you're holding back. Because you are. And this is the point.

Your team has answers. They're closer to the problems than you are. They see things you don't see. But they don't share any of this if you're filling all the space with your voice. Remember to WAIT.

WAIT: <u>WHY AM I TALKING?</u>

Before you open your mouth in a meeting, ask yourself this question. Why am I talking right now?

- Am I adding new information the team doesn't have?
- Am I asking a question to clarify something?
- Am I helping move the discussion forward?

Or am I talking because:

- I'm uncomfortable with silence?
- I want to show I'm engaged?
- I need to prove I'm the smartest person in the room?
- I'm anxious and filling space?

Most of the time, when I see leaders dominate meetings, they're talking for the wrong reasons. Not because the team needs their input. Because they need to talk.

WAIT forces you to pause. To check your motivation. To ask whether your words are helping or hurting.

Here's what I tell Visionaries: Every time you speak, you're making a choice. You're choosing to take up space. You're choosing to potentially shut down someone else who was about to speak. You're choosing to shift the energy in the room.

Make that choice intentionally. Not reflexively.

One of my favorite moments in the annual on Monday happened when the Visionary asked a question, and then he waited. He didn't jump in with his opinion. He didn't offer suggestions. He didn't start talking to fill the awkward silence.

He waited.

And you know what happened? Three people spoke up who hadn't said a word the entire meeting. They offered perspectives the Visionary hadn't considered. They identified solutions better than anything he would have come up with on his own.

Why? Because he gave them space to think.

Silence feels uncomfortable. Especially for Visionaries. You're used to filling the room with your energy, your ideas, your vision. Waiting feels passive, like you're not contributing.

But silence is a tool. When you stop talking, you create a vacuum. And somebody—usually the person who has been quiet all evening—will fill it. The person who has the answer now has an opening to share.

Your job isn't to have all the answers. Your job is to create the conditions for the team to find the answers. And sometimes, the best way to do that is to shut up.

When you start practicing WAIT, two things happen. First, you realize how often you were talking for the wrong reasons. Filling silence. Proving something. Managing your anxiety. Not actually helping.

Second, you discover your team is more capable than you thought. When you give them space, they solve problems you assumed only you could solve. They come up with ideas you wouldn't have generated on your own. They step up.

Your job as a leader isn't to be the smartest person in the room. Your job is to make sure the smartest people in the room get heard.

Ask yourself this question every time you open your mouth. You'll be shocked by how often the answer is, "I'm not sure."

Your job is to make sure the smartest people in the room get heard.

And when you can't answer the question? Close your mouth. Let someone else fill the space.

The meeting will be better for the thing.

5. Deal with the Hard Stuff

The Visionary let his best friend disrespect the entire organization for months because he didn't want the awkward conversation.

You know what's harder than one awkward conversation? Every other conversation you have after people realize you won't deal with problems.

Your team is watching what you don't do. They're grading you on the actions you avoid.

I've seen this pattern over and over: a leader knows someone isn't working out. The whole team knows someone isn't working out. But the leader waits. And waits. And waits.

Meanwhile, the rest of the team is suffering. They're picking up the slack. They're covering for the person who isn't performing. And they're watching you do nothing.

Every day you don't act, you lose credibility. Every week you let things go, trust erodes a little more.

When Jake, the CTO, finally said what everyone was thinking ("This is disrespecting our team"), it was like someone had opened a release valve. The whole room exhaled. Finally. Someone said the thing.

But here's the bottom line: Jake shouldn't have had to say anything. The Visionary should have dealt with it months earlier.

Don't be that Visionary. When you see the problem, deal with the problem. When the team brings you an issue, solve it. When someone needs to go, let them go.

Your team doesn't need you to be perfect. They need you to be decisive. They need to know when things go wrong, you'll step up and handle things.

The Visionary in the annual on Monday? He transformed his team's dynamic by saying eight words out loud: "I know I dominate meetings. Kris will help."

He didn't solve the problem by himself. He admitted a problem existed. He brought in support. And he created space for his team to step up.

By the end of day two, we'd solved three major issues that had been lingering for months. Why? Because people finally felt safe enough to speak up.

By the end of his quarterly, they'd made the hard call on his best friend. They set a timeline. They agreed on next steps. And the room felt lighter.

When you reduce power distortion, people show up differently.

The Five Dysfunctions and Your Meeting

Patrick Lencioni nailed this with his book, *The Five Dysfunctions of a Team*. The foundation is trust. Without trust, you don't have healthy conflict. Without conflict, you don't get commitment. Without commitment, there's no accountability. And without accountability, you don't get results.[22]

---

[22] Lencioni, Patrick. The Five Dysfunctions of a Team: A Leadership Fable. Jossey-Bass. 2002.

When we assessed those teams using Lencioni's "Five Dysfunctions of a Team" framework, both scored low on healthy conflict. Both were under a 7 out of 10.

Why? Because the Visionary's presence made conflict feel dangerous.

When the person with all the power is in the room, disagreeing feels risky. Even when the person says "I want healthy conflict," your nervous system is still doing the math: "If I push back too hard, will I lose my job? Will they think I'm difficult? Will they stop trusting me?"

This is why team health work is so critical. And why in annuals, I spend at least half a day on it.

People need to unpack their humanity in front of each other. They need to be vulnerable enough that when someone disagrees with them, they don't take things personally. They need to build empathy bridges so they have more direct, civil conversations.

But so often, leaders skip this step. They call empathy "the soft side" and blow by those moments. They don't let people unpack their humanity because emotional work is difficult.

But if you do this work, the rest becomes clear. Because you and I now have a bridge to the conversation. I have empathy because I understand you better. I have a more direct, civil conversation because I see you as a whole person, not a job function.

Every growing business needs healthy conflict. You know what kills healthy conflict faster than anything? A leader who punishes people for disagreeing.

And you don't have to explicitly punish them. Sometimes a look is enough. A sigh. A dismissive comment. A "well, let's move on" when someone's still talking.

Your team reads those signals. And they adjust accordingly.

What Visionaries Don't Realize About Their Impact

Here's what I wish every Visionary understood: you're never participating in a meeting. You're always influencing the thing.

Even when you're trying to be "one of the team," you're not. You don't get to be. Because everyone in the room knows you have power they don't have.

You fire them. They don't fire you. You change their compensation. They don't change yours. You veto their ideas. They don't veto yours.

This isn't a criticism. It's the reality that you must intentionally design around.

I worked with a company with a family-business dynamic. The father had built the company, and he was still transactional, command-and-control in his leadership. The son was taking over and trying to be more collaborative, more empowering.

But the team was confused. Because Dad would swoop in, make decisions, override the son, and then leave. And the son would be left trying to clean up the mess and rebuild trust.

This happened week after week until we finally got everyone in a room together and named the thing. The son looked at his father and said, "Dad, when you do this, you undermine me in front of the team. I know you're trying to help, but it's hurting us all."

The father was stunned. He had no idea. In his mind, he was "helping out" and "sharing his experience."

But the team saw things differently. They saw a leader who said one thing (the son has authority) but did another (Dad's in charge).

Once we got everything out in the open, things started to shift. The father agreed to step back more. The son agreed to escalate issues before Dad felt the need to swoop in. And the team started to trust decisions would stick.

It took months to fully rebuild the trust. But things started with one honest conversation where someone was brave enough to name the dynamic everyone else was feeling.

The Patterns I See Everywhere

After hundreds of session days with leadership teams, I've seen the same patterns play out over and over, and almost always with the same cast of characters:

The Dominant Visionary. Smart. Driven. Usually, the person with the best strategic mind in the room. Also, the person who talks the most decides the fastest and shuts down conversations without realizing it.

The Silent VP. Capable. Competent. Has good ideas but rarely shares them in meetings. Waits until afterward to express concerns. Master of the "meeting after the meeting."

The Checked-Out CTO. Was excited about the mission once. Now shows up to get through the hour. Answers questions when asked. Otherwise contributes nothing.

The Brave One. Anyone. Usually someone so secure in their role they're willing to risk the relationship to tell the truth. They're the Jake in the room. Every team needs one.

The People Pleaser. Agrees with everyone. Nods at everything. Commits to things they probably won't deliver because they don't say no. Often the source of dysfunction because they avoid conflict at all costs.

Sound familiar?

These patterns repeat because the underlying dynamic repeats: power imbalance plus lack of permission to disagree plus no process for healthy conflict equals dysfunctional meetings.

Fix those three things, and everything else gets easier.

Your Meeting Assignment

If you're a Visionary, Integrator, or another senior leader, try this at your next meeting:

Start by saying: "I know my role here changes the dynamic. Here's what I'm not here to do today: make every decision, solve every problem, or dominate the conversation. I'm here to help us think better together. Kris (or your facilitator) is going to make sure I stay in my lane. If I'm talking too much, call me on it."

Then shut up. Let the meeting run. Watch what happens when you stop being the answer and start being the space.

Your team will surprise you. I've seen this hundreds of times.

They don't need you to know everything. They need you to trust them enough to figure things out.

But here's the hard part: you have to mean the thing. You can't say "I want your input" and then override every decision. You can't say "push back on me" and then get defensive when they do. You can't say "I'm here to listen" and then spend the whole meeting talking.

Your team will test you. They'll watch to see if you're serious. The first time someone disagrees with you, the first time someone challenges your idea, the first time someone brings you bad news, is when they'll know if things are safe.

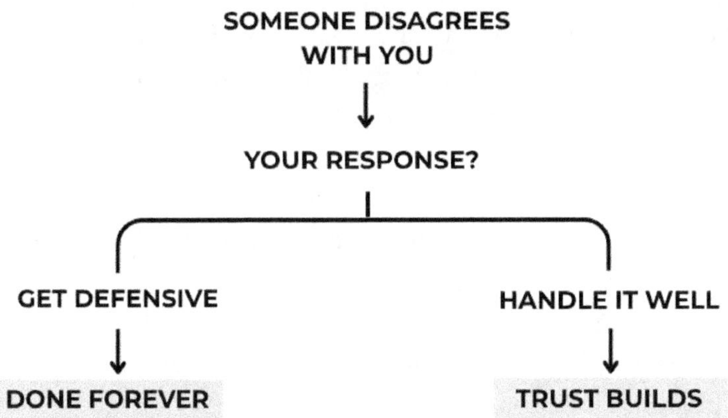

If you react badly, you're done. They'll never trust you again. They'll go right back to telling you what you want to hear.

But if you handle things well? If you thank them for the pushback? If you consider their perspective? If you change your mind when they make a good point? Things will shift.

What This Looks Like in Practice

Let me give you a practical example from one of those Monday sessions.

We were working through the Issues List. There were about six issues on there, but one was clearly the most important: they were losing market share to a competitor.

The Visionary jumped in immediately. "I think we need to drop our pricing. We're getting killed on price."

With the old dynamic, everyone would have nodded. Someone would have said, "Good idea." They'd have moved forward with a pricing change, whether it was the right move or not.

With the new dynamic, the Head of Sales raised his hand.

"I push back on this."

The Visionary paused. Then nodded. "Yeah. Go ahead."

"I don't think price is the thing. I think features are the thing. The competitor has three features we don't have. Our customers are telling us they'd pay more if we had those features. Dropping the price doesn't solve the problem."

The room waited. Would the Visionary defend his idea? Get defensive? Shut things down?

"A good point," he said. "What do the rest of you think?"

Three other people jumped in with data. Customer feedback. Market research. Deal reviews.

Turned out the Head of Sales was right. The issue was product, not price.

They made a different decision than the one the Visionary walked in with. A better decision. Because he created space for them to challenge him. This is what good facilitation, healthy conflict, and trust look like.

And things started because the Visionary was willing to be wrong.

The Hard Truth About Power

Here's what I need you to hear: if you have power in an organization, you won't escape it. You won't be able to pretend the thing doesn't exist. You can't wish it away.

Your title gives you gravity. Your position gives you weight. Your voice carries more than other voices. The question is: what are you going to do with this power?

Are you going to use it to make yourself feel important? To prove you're the smartest person in the room? To win every argument?

Or are you going to use your influence to create space for others? To elevate different perspectives? To build a team stronger than you are?

The best leaders I've worked with understand this. They know they have power. They acknowledge the thing. And then they consciously choose to distribute it. They don't dominate. They facilitate. They don't solve. They empower. They don't talk. They listen.

And their teams are better because of it.

The worst leaders I've worked with? They pretend they don't have power. They say things like "I'm one of the team" while simultaneously overriding every decision. They claim they want input while making it clear that disagreement is dangerous.

That is nothing more than manipulation, and your team sees through it. They always do.

Before we wrap up this chapter, remember that presence has power. Use it wisely.

Show up fully or don't show up at all. If you're half in and half out, you're creating confusion. The seagull leader damages culture faster than almost anything else.

Name the power dynamic. Tell them what you're not there to do. Bring in help if you need help. And for the love of all things productive, put your phone away.

Show up fully or don't show up at all.

Meetings don't break because people are incompetent. They break because power isn't distributed well.

You have the title. You have the authority. Now create the space for others to use theirs.

And when someone finally speaks up (when they tell you the hard truth you need to hear), thank them. Even if things sting. Especially if things sting.

Because this is the moment when your team decides if they trust you.

The moment when your meetings start working.

The moment when your culture starts to heal.

Don't waste it.

"Meetings Suck Less" Realization

The moment you admit that your presence changes the room is the moment the room changes. Stop pretending you're "one of the team." You're not. Own the power you have. Then give it away in the meeting. This is how you build leaders who don't need you to function.

Next up: I invited my colleague, Dr. Audra Stanton, M.D., to join me in discussing the psychological factors contributing to what I see in session rooms, such as why we show up the way we do in meetings and why they can so easily bring us down.

6

THE PSYCHOLOGY OF MEETINGS BY AUDRA STANTON, M.D.

I was honored and excited when Kris asked me to be a contributor to this book, as I am a strong believer in the power of EOS and have tremendous respect for those in the community who help companies implement and execute EOS well. I am also passionate about the human factor that affects meetings and how those dynamics play out. I want to share a little about me before we jump in.

I am the Head of Product at Ninety. Before I entered the tech world as an innovator, I was a practicing physician and an educator. I have published research in scientific journals in the areas of neuroscience, medical training, and the learning curves people engage in order to adapt to new situations and achieve new knowledge they can successfully apply. I have built and led large cross-functional product teams in tech and have been featured in various publications such as *Forbes, Emotional Intelligence Magazine,* and *Training Magazine* regarding the future of work and how humans create meaning through what they do. I understand both the science of how people learn, think, and process information, and the messy reality of getting humans to work together.

I've learned that meetings are where psychology meets reality. Where your brain's response to feedback collides with your fear of judgment. Where relationship dynamics shape what gets said and what stays buried.

Most people think meetings suck because of bad agendas or too many people. Those things matter. But the biggest problem with most is psychological. And nobody talks about this.

So I sat down with Kris Snyder, a Professional EOS Implementer who's facilitated over 400 session days with 50-plus clients. If anyone has seen the psychology of meetings play out in real time, over and over, across different teams and industries, he has.

What follows is what we uncovered together. The patterns. The dynamics. The things happening under the surface that make your meetings better or worse.

Why Your Brain Is Already on Alert

Here's something most facilitators miss: your brain treats meetings as potential threats.

Given the brain's natural unease with change and its habit of taking even well-meant feedback to heart, traditional methods often make learning feel more pressure-filled than needed.

Walk into a meeting where you're supposed to give feedback or solve problems. Your brain goes into alert mode. Is this safe? Will I get judged? Am I about to hear something to make me feel bad?

And if the meeting only happens once a quarter, or once a year? The pressure is massive. Everything rides on this one conversation. Your brain goes into high alert.

This is why Kris does what he does at the start of every meeting.

> Kris: "One of the reasons I love the segue and the check-in is to slow things down. Because you're often coming in with carryover from whatever moment you were in before, so you come in hot. You'll hear me joke about this sometimes when I start a meeting. I'm like, hey team, I'm coming in hot, right? Because whatever momentum was happening in the last meeting, I know I gotta shift gears."

He's doing something most people don't recognize: he's lowering the psychological threat. He's signaling to everyone's brain: this is safe. We're human. We're in this together.

> Kris: "So we go around, and we create the empathy triggers. Personal, professional best. You've seen me do one-word opens. I'll start a meeting and ask about the favorite meeting of the day, trying to get people thinking about the topic we're about to dig into."

The segue and check-in aren't fluff. These are psychological tools. You're pulling people out of wherever they were. You're realigning them with the humans in the room. You're lowering the threat response before you get to the hard stuff.

The Relationship Layer Nobody Sees

People assume they know what's going on in meetings. Most of the time, they don't. Because they're not thinking about things from other people's perspectives.

Every person has a different relationship with every other person. Your motivations and my motivations. Why we're in the room. What we're doing. What we're trying to accomplish. There's an easier way of executing when this is clear. And the danger element is stronger the more people are in the room.

When I first started working at Ninety, one of my direct reports noted this as we went into a call. She said, "You're different in some meetings than in other meetings."

I told her, "Yeah, because sometimes it's only you and me in a meeting, and sometimes it's eighteen other people meeting, and I only know a quarter of them."

The way you show up is impacted by the relationship status you have with the people in the group.

And so if there are people you don't know very well, you might be thinking to yourself, "What do they think of me right now? Do they know what my job is? Do they know why I'm here?" And this changes the way you decide to engage, depending on who's around you.

We see this a lot in companies. When I'm in a series of different meetings with different people, there's a different version of me that people experience. At the same time, I experience a different version of some of those people whom I've met with in other meetings as well.

This is the truth nobody talks about: you're not showing up as one consistent person across all meetings. You're adjusting. Adapting. Reading the room. And everyone else is doing the same thing.

Kris gets this. He uses known work style tendencies and factors to make these dynamics visible.

Kris: "I also love one of the things about the digital side of meetings. I get to see people's Kolbe, their Type Coach, their Enneagram constantly. So if I'm trying to remember the thing, this helps. I was in a session the other day where there was a 10 in the room and a 3, and they were not having things. They were so disconnected. And then you're like, okay, so this is why this is happening. I even said this to them. I'm like, okay, let's slow down for a minute. You're 10, you're 3, you're completely okay with ambiguity and speed, and you are not. So let's figure this out together."

The more visible you make these dynamics, the less energy people spend wondering what everyone else is thinking. The less they're managing the relationship dynamics while trying to focus on the agenda.

The Math of Group Dynamics

Here's the math: The more people you have in a meeting, the more complicated the dynamics are.

As the call gets bigger, all of a sudden, everything you say has a lot more weight. Your words fall on many more sets of ears, so there's a lot more potential for judgment of you if something you say doesn't land.

More ears, more weight. More potential for judgment. This is what people are feeling when they're in big meetings. This is why people clam up. This is why the same three people dominate while everyone else stays quiet.

And if you have any natural insecurity in your seat at all, and you're saying something in front of people who are more senior than you, or in a department you're less familiar with, the psychological weight of speaking up is massive.

Kris sees this playing out in different ways.

Kris: "The group dynamics are weird. I find on the quieter side, the introverts, the feeling people on the Myers-Briggs, the feelers, right, need to be pulled in. If you're not making space for them or slowing down for them, they won't participate. They won't do the thing. And then you'll miss the thing from them. You're missing one of the perspectives needed to be healthier. I think everyone should speak in a Level 10 during IDS. Everybody, every time."

He also sees people showing up with different tools. We have Luke, who comes into every meeting and always uses the hammer instead of the other tools available to him in his toolbox. The fine-tuning tools just never get used, and sometimes the meeting doesn't call for the hammer. People are seeing him use the hammer all the time and thinking, "Oh man, this guy always shows up this way, and it's making things hard. Should I use the hammer too, or should I stand back and watch the hammer go to town?"

There are other people who kind of change and vary what tools they decide to use. They might use the screwdriver, they might use the wrench, or the needle-nosed pliers, depending on who's in the room and what the discussion topics are.

Some people are all hammer, all the time. Other people read the room and adjust. Both create dynamics you have to manage as a facilitator.

This is the work of facilitation. Seeing the patterns. Naming them. Redirecting them before they poison the meeting.

Why People Don't Speak Up

Sometimes people think, well, this is a me problem, probably something no one else cares about. So I don't know if I should say anything. I don't know if this is appropriate for me to bring up. People will think less of me if I put this issue on the table, because everyone else knows the answer to this, and I'm the only one who thinks this is important, or the only one who doesn't.

This is the inner monologue running in most people's heads during meetings. The fear of judgment. The fear of looking stupid. The fear of being the only one who doesn't get it.

Half the time, everyone else has the same problem. Everyone else is wondering the same thing. But nobody says anything because they all think they're the only one.

As a facilitator, it is challenging when people hold back, especially when they do so out of fear that one or more people in the room are going to judge them based on what they say. Creating a safety net helps people feel it's ok to put issues out there, so that even things they may be hesitant about or perceive as "stupid" questions, they feel confident in raising without fear or shame.

This is what separates good facilitators from bad ones. Bad facilitators think their job is managing the agenda. Good facilitators know their job is creating the safety net.

Kris does this explicitly.

Kris: " I don't say this often, but when I feel like a team is holding back, I want to remind them that giving your opinion in this meeting is what you are being paid to do. And if you have an important thing to say, you gotta say it. I don't know where the thing is going to go in the end, but I'd rather have you put it out there and for us to deal with than hold back."

He also does this through how he responds.

> Kris: "And when someone does bring up 'the stupid question'? I validate the hell out of the thing. 'Great question. I'm glad you asked.' Because I want everyone else in the room to see: this is safe. You're allowed to ask. You're allowed to not know. You're allowed to be human."

This is how you create psychological safety. Not through policies. Through how you respond in the moment.

Vulnerable Leadership as a Skill

Leaders need to be intentionally taught how to embrace and communicate vulnerability. There's a long-standing misconception that admitting mistakes or sharing decision-making struggles somehow weakens authority. In reality, this does the opposite.

When I work with new teams, I talk openly about a lesson I've learned the hard way. I share a miscommunication that missed the mark, or a bad decision and its consequences. Doing this immediately flattens the hierarchy and communicates, "We are all human here, and we are in this together." The most approachable leaders earn trust by not being perfect, but by being human.

Vulnerability isn't a personality trait reserved for a select few who choose to wear their heart on their sleeve. Vulnerability is a learnable leadership skill directly elevating engagement, fostering belonging, and prioritizing growth and acceptance across a team.

Kris models this at the start of meetings.

> Kris: "This is what I'm doing when I say 'I'm coming in hot' at the start of a meeting. I'm being vulnerable. I'm admitting I'm not perfectly composed. I'm human. And this signals to everyone else: you're allowed to be human too."

When leaders hide their struggles, hide their uncertainties, and hide their mistakes, what message does this send? The message is: you'd better hide yours, too. And then you get meetings where nobody says what they're thinking. Where everyone's performing. Where the real issues stay buried.

You want psychological safety in your meetings? Start by being vulnerable yourself.

When You Become Someone's Baggage

I am a big fan of trying my best to not be part of someone else's baggage from their work. And sometimes you can't avoid this as a leader, as someone the person works with on a regular basis.

Not being part of someone's baggage is the goal. But…you're going to f*ck up sometimes. You're going to lose your cool. You're going to say something you shouldn't say. You're going to criticize someone in a meeting when you should have pulled them aside separately.

And when this happens, you have a choice. Let's say you do end up criticizing someone in a meeting in a public way, emotions are running high. It's critically important after this happens to acknowledge you f*cked up, and tell the person you were in the wrong and you're sorry with no excuses. Because this will be a part of their memory of the circumstance, and it won't be just the bad stuff.

"Oh, yeah, Alexander did this, and then he let things go and pretended like this was nothing." Guess what? They're gonna carry that with them, and then it becomes part of their baggage. It lives with them as they do other things in their work and life. These things can be challenging for people to let go of.

Additionally, when other people, who weren't on the receiving end of this conflict, see what is happening, they ask themselves, "Is this how we do things here at this company? Is this okay?" And without the person also acknowledging to the group, "Hey, I did this thing, I shouldn't have done this, this wasn't okay," they all walk away with this wrong idea that it's the right thing to do.

The observers. The people watching. They're taking notes. They're learning what's acceptable by what's modeled. And if you don't call out your own behavior, if you don't acknowledge you were wrong, they think: this is how we do things here.

And then you've created a culture where people think losing your cool is acceptable. Where public criticism is acceptable.

Kris told me about a time this happened to him.

Kris: "I had one quarterly last year where there was a topic that had been brought up multiple times. I felt like the thing got answered. And then the person brought the thing up again. And I lost my cool. I was like, there's no new way to answer this question, and you don't like the answer. And I went off. I should not have done it, because there were too many people on the call.

"I went up to the person after and apologized. I said, 'Hey, this was not appropriate. I'm frustrated. I need to know why you're doing this. Because I don't want to keep doing this. I think we close the gap, and then you pull it back open. I know my reaction was inappropriate.'

"So then, after the break, when we started, I needed to own up to it so the team knew I was in the wrong. I needed to acknowledge to them that my behavior was inappropriate and ridiculous. What are the reasons why I did what I did? Doesn't matter, other than I did something that wasn't cool, and we should know that's not the right behavior to model. Please don't do this. I was in the wrong, and I'll be better next time.

"Then I needed to clear the air. This was not cool. I shouldn't have done this. Let's talk about where we're at, because there's something going on not being talked about between us, and this took place in a meeting, and we don't need this to happen again."

Kris calls this a clear-the-air meeting.

There's so often unsaid emotional stuff. What's being talked about during the meeting is not the root cause or the real issue that needs discussed, as we talk about a lot in EOS with issues. There is an issue, but the issue is not stated or is not clear to either party. And sometimes this comes out as a dramatic moment of conflict.

The surface issue wasn't the real issue. The real issue was underneath. Unstated. And because you didn't address the real issue, it kept coming back. And people get exhausted. And when people get exhausted, they do emotional things.

If the issue still doesn't get handled, it keeps brewing until it becomes a chronic dynamic of the meeting. Underlying tension. Unresolved conflict. And this poisons every future meeting.

If something like this does happen, the follow-through is crucial. It shows a lot about the person's character, also, to come to the realization that "Hey, this wasn't me at my best, I'm sorry, and this is not gonna happen again."

The follow-through. The apology. The acknowledgment. This is what keeps you from becoming someone's baggage. This is what models the right behavior for the observers. This is what clears the air, so you solve the real issue.

You're going to f*ck up. Accept this. But when you do, own your mistake. Apologize to the person. Acknowledge the thing to the team. Clear the air. Get to the real issue.

This is how you stop being someone's baggage and start being someone who creates healthy meeting dynamics.

Why Structure Helps Humans

The great thing about the EOS tools is that even with the most complex personality makeup and motivation level you have in a room, everybody is able to try and focus on a task, so they kind of put aside some of the emotional weight of how they're feeling in the moment.

The structure doesn't replace the human element. The structure creates space for the human element to come through.

Without structure, you get chaos. People talking over each other. Meetings running long. Issues never getting solved. And all the emotional weight, all the relationship dynamics, all the fear and insecurity, fills the space.

With structure, you give people a framework. You give them roles. You give them a process for getting through the hard stuff. And this lowers the cognitive load. People spend less energy wondering how to participate and more energy participating.

Kris saw this play out with a team he coached.

> Kris: "I had a team I stopped coaching in 2023. The CEO called me up one day, saying, 'Hey, I need a quarterly. You're only going to know three of the seven people because we've got four new people in there.'
>
> "So now I don't know what I'm walking into. But the company grew a lot, so when they upskilled, new leaders from bigger companies came in to keep this new thing growing. Because most of these folks had been hired recently, they were familiar with L10s but hadn't yet seen a quarterly. They were EOS-aware, but hadn't experienced facilitated EOS before.
>
> "So we started to go through this whole thing, and at some point, we came back from a break, and they told me, 'I have sat in so many meetings, but never one where there is structure like this.'"

This was the type of structure that helps humanity shine.

> Kris: "And it's very human. The structure's helping me as a human come through in the meeting, versus structure for structure's sake and process. It's very humanized in how we approach this. And then after we do it, super efficient, and the way in which things are getting navigated around the room, the meeting itself becomes so much better."

The takeaway is that both structure and humanity come out of EOS. It is human in how we do the thing, and yet we still are highly efficient. We're productive in how we run these meetings. And often, if you came from a bigger company, you didn't have either one of those. Meetings weren't productive, facilitated, or structured, and they didn't feel human at all.

The structure doesn't replace the human element. The structure creates space for the human element to come through.

TSP: Simple? Yes. Easy? No.

TSP stands for Truthful, Specific, Positive. We use this framework for providing feedback. TSP is simple, yes, but that doesn't make it easy.

> Kris: "The truthful part is you have to say what you're thinking. Not what you think people want to hear. What you're thinking.
>
> "The specific part means you have to give examples. No conjecture. No theory. Examples.
>
> "The positive part is you have to frame things with a growth mindset. Not tearing down. Building up."

And all three of these things are hard. Especially in a room where you're worried about judgment, or power dynamics, or relationships.

Think back to what I said earlier about complex relationships. When you're in a meeting with people more senior than you, or in a department you're less familiar with, or with people you don't know well? Being truthful, specific, and positive gets even harder. Because you're managing the content of what you're saying AND the relationship dynamics AND your own insecurity.

If you don't do TSP, you won't get to real issues.

But if you don't do TSP, you won't get to real issues. You can dance around them, but nothing ever gets solved.

Because the alternative to TSP is sitting in meetings where nothing real gets said. Where people nod along. Where issues stay buried. Where you leave thinking the same thing you thought walking in.

And those meetings? Those are the ones making people miserable.

What You Need to Do

Here's where Kris and I landed in terms of the biggest takeaways on meeting psychology.

People show up to meetings carrying momentum from wherever they were before. You need to slow things down at the start. Segue. Check-in. Get people out of whatever they were in.

You need to be clear on the objective. Why are we here? What are we solving? If people don't know this, they won't show up right.

You need to know who's in the room. Their personalities. Their seat. Why they're there. And their relationships with each other. Because people show up differently depending on who else is there. They're asking themselves, "What do they think of me? Do they know why I'm here?" And all of this is happening while you're trying to run the meeting.

You need to make space for everyone to speak. Go around the room. Pull people in. Don't let the extroverts dominate. Don't let the introverts hide. Remember, the bigger the meeting, the more weight every word carries. The more potential for judgment. The more people will hold back.

You need to call out the patterns that aren't working. The hammer when the meeting needs needle-nosed pliers. The dominating. The holding back. Redirect when you see this happening.

You need to create psychological safety. Make people feel like they put things out there without getting judged. This is the hardest part. And the most important part.

And you need structure to make this all possible. Not structure for structure's sake. Structure serving the humans in the room. Structure helping people put aside the emotional weight and focus on the task. Structure creating space for the human element to come through.

When you do these things, meetings stop being theater, and they start being the place where real work gets done. Where people feel heard. Where issues get solved. Where people build their sense of meaning and identity at work.

This is the psychology of meetings. Understanding what's happening beneath the surface. Understanding the relationship dynamics. Understanding the fear and insecurity. Understanding the different versions of people showing up depending on who's in the room. And creating the conditions for people to bring their best.

It isn't complicated. But it's hard to execute. And worth every bit of effort.

"Meetings Suck Less" Realization

The way people show up to meetings is shaped by momentum from before, clarity on the objective, who else is in the room, and whether they feel safe speaking up. It's the responsibility of every person in a meeting to create and maintain the conditions that allow people to bring their best. Slow things down at the start. Make the objective clear. Know the personalities and seats in the room. Pull everyone in. Call out patterns that are not working. Build psychological safety. Use structure to serve the humans, not the other way around. When you do this, meetings stop being something people endure and start being the place where real work happens.

Up next: When meetings suck, culture is negatively impacted. Let's talk about the ripple effects of meeting dysfunction and how to rebuild trust when things are already gone.

7

WHEN MEETINGS SUCK, CULTURE BREAKS

You can fix your meeting structure. You can implement Level 10 Meetings. You can use IDS religiously. You can rate every meeting from one to ten. You can do everything we have already discussed to try to make your meetings suck less.

But if trust is broken, none of this matters. Meetings are where culture lives. It's at meetings that you can evaluate whether your team believes what leadership says and whether they feel safe enough to tell the truth.

When meetings are healthy, culture is healthy. When meetings break, culture breaks. And the damage spreads fast.

Let me show you what this looks like in real time.

When Trust Gets Shaken

I had a call with Sam earlier today. The numbers coming out of his area have not been what we need. Not even close.

I've been flying high on this one, trusting the process, staying out of the weeds. But I can't stay out of it anymore. The results aren't there. So I'm coming in. Not to micromanage. Not to take over. But to understand what's blocking us and figure out how we get to where we agreed we'd be.

> Sam started explaining. *Kate did this. Bennett did this. There are roadblocks.*
>
> I stop him. "Succeed or escalate. We agreed as a team that we were going to hit this a certain goal, so if you're not getting what you need, how are we going to get there?"
>
> Here's the thing: my objective wasn't to call Sam out. I was calling him up. We agreed on an output. I own the thing if the output doesn't get delivered, so I need to know what's in the way. And we need to solve it.
>
> But I also know how Sam might have experienced the conversation. If he walked out thinking, "Snyder's all up in my stuff," he wouldn't be wrong.

When trust gets shaken, I inspect. You inspect. We all inspect.

This is how things happen. You expect something. You trust someone to deliver. And they don't.

Not because they're incompetent. Not because they don't care. There are legitimate roadblocks. The goal was unrealistic. Communication broke down somewhere.

But the result is the same: Your trust gets shaken.

And now? You start inspecting. You ask for more updates. You check in more frequently. You want to see the work. You hover.

You're not trying to micromanage. You're trying to course correct. But the inspection feels like lack of trust to the person on the receiving end.

They feel smothered. They perform worse under the scrutiny. This confirms your suspicion that something's off. So you inspect more. And the cycle spirals.

This is where meeting culture starts to break. The one-on-ones that used to be collaborative problem-solving sessions are now status reports. The team member is defending their work instead of getting help removing obstacles. You're frustrated they're not delivering. They're frustrated you don't trust them. Nobody's solving the issue.

Breaking the Cycle

Here's how you stop the spiral: Name the issue out loud in your next one-on-one.

"I realize I've been checking in more frequently. This probably feels like I don't trust you. Here's what happened: We agreed to deliver X by Y date, and we're not on track. I need to understand why so we can fix this together. What's blocking us?"

Frame the thing as support, not scrutiny. You're there to remove obstacles, not to judge. You're there to succeed together.

You can't fix things if you don't talk about things.

And then listen. There are roadblocks you didn't know about. Your expectations were unrealistic. There's a skill gap needing addressing.

The point is that you can't fix things if you don't talk about things. And you can't talk about things if your meetings aren't safe enough to be honest.

The Transition Tax[IP]

Companies don't grow in a straight line. You might progress from early-stage startup to medium-sized business and eventually get to your goal of becoming a mature, high-revenue company, but there's always a transition between those stages. And people feel the weight of that transition.

I'm working with a company where a group of people came in together from a previous organization. They had history. They had shorthand. They had each other. The existing team? They felt replaced in their own house. They even made up a word for the experience. You know culture has a problem when your people are creating vocabulary to describe how bad things feel.

Does it matter if we know exactly what happened? Not a whole lot. What matters is how they experienced the thing.

And now there's a trust problem. The legacy team doesn't trust the new leadership. The new leaders feel resistance from the old guard. Meetings have become passive-aggressive performances where nobody says what they're thinking.

One person on the team told me the team has a deep desire to be trusted by the Visionary. At the same time, they are concerned he doesn't trust them. They think he needs to know every little thing they're doing. He micromanages the process.

I asked if this was true. The person said, "I don't think this is true today. But similar issues were true before."

Bingo. Here's the hangover from the transition. The perception hasn't caught up to the reality. The Visionary changed his approach. But the team is still operating from the old playbook.

This is what happens when companies don't handle transitions well. The damage lingers. Trust erodes slowly, meeting by meeting, until nobody believes anything the leadership says.

Why Transitions Break Meeting Culture

Think about what happens during a reorg or leadership change: People lose their seats. Or they keep their seats but lose their authority. New people come in from the outside with fancy titles and bigger paychecks. The folks who built the company from scratch feel like second-class citizens.

Nobody talks about things directly. But everyone feels them. And where does the backlash show up? In meetings.

The legacy people stop contributing ideas. Why bother? The new regime has already decided. The new people get frustrated by the resistance. Why won't these people get on board? Leadership wonders why execution is dragging.

And underneath all this lies the true problem: broken trust. The fix isn't complicated. But the fix requires courage.

You have to name the transition. Acknowledge what people experienced. Talk about how the change felt. Create space for the grief, the anger, the confusion.

Then you rebuild. Slowly. Meeting by meeting. Conversation by conversation.

Most struggling teams aren't at a 7 or above in the dysfunction of healthy conflict. They're at a 5. A 6 on a good day.

And where do you see this most clearly? In meetings. You see it when people don't speak up. When issues get tabled instead of solved. When the same problems resurface week after week because nobody wants to enter the danger.

You don't build trust in a broken meeting. But you also don't fix the business without healthy meetings. It's a loop, and the only way out is to start somewhere.

I'm planning a team health session with the team struggling with the Transition Tax. We're going to start by talking about trust at a high level. Making things personal right away is too hard. Instead, we'll talk about what trust looks like in companies generally. Rate some scenarios. Get comfortable with the language.

Once they're comfortable talking about trust in the abstract, we'll make things personal by talking about trust on this team. What's working. What's not. Where the gaps are.

You don't start with the hard stuff. You build up to it. You create safety first. Then you go deep.

Rebuilding Trust in the Room

So how do you rebuild meeting trust when things have been broken? First, name the breach in trust. Out loud. In the meeting. "I know there's tension here. I know some of you feel like you got pushed aside during the transition. Let's talk about this."

Second, create space for people to talk. Not fake "open door policy" talk. Real talk. Use IDS. Pull out the Issues List. Say, "What are we not saying?"

Third, if you're the leader who broke the trust (even unintentionally), you go first. Acknowledge where things went wrong. Admit when communication broke down. Ask for feedback. Then (and this is the hardest part) listen without getting defensive.

When Sam walked out of our conversation today thinking I'm all up in his stuff, he wasn't entirely wrong. I am more involved than I was. But I can either let this sit there and fester, or I can name the thing next time we talk.

"Hey, I know I've been checking in more. This probably feels different. Here's why. And here's what I need from you so we get back to where we were."

Leadership is not pretending the dynamic doesn't exist. Leaders acknowledge the issue and work through it.

Fourth, focus on evidence. Ask: "Why do you think I don't trust you?" Then listen to the evidence. Maybe the accusation is grounded, or maybe it's just a matter of perception. Either way, you have to address the thing.

If the team thinks the Visionary doesn't trust them, I need them to tell me why. What's the evidence? What behaviors are they seeing? What are they interpreting?

Either the Visionary is trying to remove obstacles, and they're experiencing micromanagement, or the Visionary is micromanaging because his trust got shaken in the past. Either way, we don't fix things until we name them.

The Quarterly Conversation as a Trust Tool

Here's a practical tip: use Quarterly Conversations to rebuild trust at the individual level.

As you sit down with each person on your team, connect with them about what is working, what isn't, and what sort of support they need. This is where trust gets built. Not in the big all-hands meeting. Not in the company-wide email. In the quiet one-on-one where you listen.

If you're trying to rebuild trust after a reorg, after a tough year, after a leadership change, start here. One person at a time. Quarterly. Consistently.

And here's a tip: use the TSP framework for feedback. Truthful. Specific. Positive.

True means you're honest. Not brutal. Honest. You say what needs to be said.

Specific means you don't use generalities. No "always" or "never" or "forever." Those are trigger words. They're not accurate, and they shut people down. Be specific about what you observed and when.

Positive tone will help them hear what you're saying. If you're negative, if you're attacking, people shut down. Frame it in a way that invites growth, not defensiveness.

Let me give you an example. Say someone on your team keeps missing deadlines. Here's the wrong way to give feedback:

"You never deliver on time. You're always behind. This is becoming a pattern."

Always. Never. Pattern. Those words trigger defensiveness immediately. The person stops listening and starts preparing their defense.

Here's the TSP way:

"I noticed the Q3 marketing plan came in three days late, and last week's customer analysis was delayed by two days. I'm concerned we're building a trend impacting the team's ability to plan. What's getting in the way? How do I help you hit deadlines more consistently?"

True: The facts are accurate. Specific: Exact examples with dates. Positive: Framed as "how do we solve this" instead of "you're failing."

This kind of feedback lands. You create conversation instead of confrontation. And over time, you rebuild trust.

Trust isn't rebuilt in a single grand gesture. It takes dozens of small, consistent actions over time. Quarterly Conversations are one of those actions.

The Cost of Avoiding Conflict

Let me tell you what happens when teams avoid conflict in meetings. In the short term, it feels peaceful. Everyone's nice. Nobody rocks the boat. Meetings end on time with minimal discomfort.

In the long term, the business suffers. Because all those issues you're not addressing? They don't disappear. They compound.

The product roadmap nobody questions, even though the thing's headed in the wrong direction. The hire everybody knows is wrong, but nobody wants to say the thing. The strategy shift that sounds great on paper, but makes no sense to the people doing the work. All of this stays buried. Until things don't.

And then the business hits a ceiling. Revenue stalls. Key people leave. The board starts asking hard questions. And suddenly, all those avoided conflicts come flooding back at once.

Now you're having ten hard conversations instead of one. And the trust helping you navigate them gracefully doesn't exist anymore.

Patrick Lencioni calls this the absence of trust. When trust is absent, people won't engage in healthy conflict. They'll avoid the thing. Smooth things over. Pretend agreement. In the meeting, everyone is performing their role. Nobody's solving anything.

This is death by a thousand cuts. The business doesn't die all at once. It dies slowly, issue by issue, meeting by meeting, as teams avoid the conversations mattering.

And why do they avoid them? Usually because trust is broken. Because last time someone spoke up, they got shut down. Or ignored. Or worse, retaliated against. So they stop speaking up. And the meetings become theater.

I've seen leadership teams score themselves at a 5 or 6 on healthy conflict. Not good enough. High-performing teams are at a 7 or above. They disagree productively. They challenge each other's ideas. They make decisions faster because they're not avoiding the debate.

But you don't manufacture this overnight. You have to build the foundation first. And the foundation is trust.

What Trust Looks Like in Meetings

Here's how you know if trust exists in your meetings:

People speak up early. They don't wait until after the meeting to share their real opinions in the parking lot. They say what they think in the room, while there's still time to do something about the thing.

Disagreement doesn't feel personal. When someone challenges your idea, you don't get defensive. You get curious. You ask questions. You want to understand their perspective.

Silence means agreement. Not performance. When nobody speaks up after you ask, "Any concerns?" it's because there aren't any, not because people are afraid to share them.

Issues get solved, not tabled. When something comes up, the team leans in. They use IDS. They identify the root cause, discuss thoroughly, and solve the thing. They don't punt to next week.

People admit mistakes. Without fear of retribution. "I screwed this up. Here's what happened. Here's how we fix this."

Meetings end with clarity. Everyone knows what was decided, who owns what, and by when. No confusion. No "Wait, what did we decide?" conversations after the fact.

If your meetings don't look like this, you've got a trust problem. And this trust problem is breaking your culture.

HEALTHY MEETING CULTURE	**BROKEN MEETING CULTURE**
✓ People speak up early (not in parking lot after)	✗ Real opinions come out after meeting
✓ Disagreement doesn't feel personal	✗ Coded language and dancing around issues
✓ Silence means actual agreement	✗ Silence means fear, not agreement
✓ Issues get solved, not tabled	✗ Same issues every week
✓ People admit mistakes without fear	✗ CYA behavior dominates
✓ Meetings end with clarity	✗ "Wait, what did we decide?" confusion

Rate Your Meetings (No, For Real)

Remember the meeting rating? This tool can help build trust as well. The rating forces accountability. If you're consistently giving your meetings a six, you have to answer: why? What made this a six instead of an eight? What would make things better?

And here's what's great about this: you don't have to fake the thing. Not for long, anyway.

If trust is broken, people will keep rating meetings low. Because broken trust means unresolved issues. Which means meetings aren't solving anything. Which means low ratings.

The ratings become the diagnostic tool. They show you where the pain is. And they force the conversation about fixing it.

I've had teams where one person consistently rates meetings lower than everyone else. This person is usually seeing something the rest of the team is missing. They don't feel heard. Their issues keep getting tabled. They fundamentally disagree with the direction but don't feel safe speaking up.

The low rating is a signal. And if you're smart, you follow up with the person, saying, "Hey, I notice you've rated the last three meetings at a five or six. Talk to me. What's not working? What do you need to see to get to an eight?"

This question unlocks the real conversation. The one you've been avoiding. The one keeping your culture stuck.

The 7-Step Recovery Plan: Practical Steps

So let's say you recognize your meeting culture is broken. Trust is low. People are avoiding conflict. Issues aren't getting solved. What do you do?

Here's a recovery plan:

Step 1: Name things publicly.

Call a meeting. Not a regular weekly. A special one. Say: "I think our meeting culture is broken. Trust is low. We're not solving real issues. And I want to fix this. But I can't fix things alone. We have to fix things together."

This will be uncomfortable. Do it anyway.

Step 2: Get specific about the problem.

Don't let things stay abstract. Ask: "What specifically isn't working? What do you experience in our meetings making you not want to speak up?"

Write down what people say. All of the things. Don't defend. Don't explain. Listen and capture.

Step 3: Own your part.

If you're the leader, you probably contributed to the problem. You dominated conversations. You shut someone down once, and they never forgot the thing. You've been avoiding hard decisions.

Own it. Out loud. "I realize I've been checking in too much, and this feels like micromanagement. This is on me. Here's what I'm going to change."

Step 4: Create new agreements.

What do you want your meetings to look like? What behaviors do you want to see more of? Less of?

Make agreements. Write them down. Post them in the room.

"We agree to speak up in the meeting, not in the parking lot afterward." "We agree to challenge ideas, not people." "We agree to use IDS when issues surface instead of tabling them."

Whatever you need. Make things explicit.

Step 5: Use the tools religiously.

Hold a Level 10 Meeting on the same day and at the same time every week. Use IDS for issues. No exceptions. Rate the meeting every single time. Schedule Quarterly Conversations with every direct report.

The tools create structure. Structure creates safety. Safety creates trust.

Step 6: Track improvement.

How are your meeting ratings trending? Are they going up? Are issues getting solved faster? Are people speaking up more? Are sidebar conversations decreasing?

Track the signals. Celebrate progress. Call out backsliding.

Step 7: Be patient.

Trust takes time to rebuild. You won't fix a year of broken culture in a month. But you will see progress if you're consistent.

Quarter by quarter, the ratings will improve. Issues will be solved more cleanly. People will start believing that speaking up won't get them punished.

When you see these signs, you know you're winning.

Culture Lives in the Room

Here's the bottom line: culture is what happens in the room when things get hard. Do people speak up, or do they shut down? Do leaders listen, or do they defend? Do teams solve issues, or do they let them fester?

Meetings are where culture lives. When meetings are healthy, culture is healthy. When meetings break, culture breaks. And when culture breaks, good people leave. The best people leave first, because they have options. They're not going to stick around in a place where their voice doesn't matter, where real issues never get solved, where perception from two years ago still drives behavior today.

When meetings are healthy, culture is healthy.

You lose talent. You lose momentum. You lose trust.

And all of this shows up first in your meetings.

The team I'm working with that has all of those people who worked together at a previous org? If we don't fix the meeting culture, the legacy people who feel cast aside will leave. They'll take their institutional knowledge, their relationships, their understanding of the business, and the company will be worse off.

The same thing is true in your company. Whatever trust issues are lurking—micromanagement, transition trauma, or broken commitments—they are all showing up in your meetings. Fix the meetings, and you start fixing the culture.

Start Somewhere

Before we wrap this chapter, here are a few reminders. Fixing culture through meetings isn't a one-time thing. It's a discipline.

You have to show up. Every week. Same time. Issues List ready. Everyone accountable.

You have to rate your meetings. One to ten. Every time. And when you're at a six, you talk about why and what needs to change.

You have to use the tools: IDS for solving issues, Rocks for quarterly priorities, Scorecards for tracking what matters, and the Accountability Chart so everyone knows their seat.

This is the EOS rhythm. Do this enough times, and healthy meetings become the norm. Skip this for a few weeks, and dysfunction creeps back in.

Start with one meeting. Your leadership team. Your direct reports. Wherever you have influence. Name the trust issues. Create space for honest conversation. Use the tools consistently. Rate your meetings. And watch what happens when people realize they can finally speak up.

If your meetings are breaking, your culture is breaking. Simple. And serious. But the good news? Meetings are fixable. Culture is fixable. You have to be willing to do the hard work of acknowledging what's broken and committing to fixing the thing.

Trust needs rebuilding after a transition. Patterns of inspection need to shift back to expectation. Perceptions from the past need updating to match today's reality.

Whatever the thing is, start with your next meeting. Name what's broken. Create space for honesty. Use IDS to solve the real issues. Give feedback using TSP (true, specific, positive).

And be patient. Trust rebuilds one conversation at a time. One meeting at a time. One quarter at a time.

Your meetings are where your culture lives. Make them count.

"Meetings Suck Less" Realization

When trust breaks, we inspect. When we inspect without naming the thing, teams experience micromanagement. When teams feel micromanaged, they perform worse. Which makes us inspect more. And the spiral continues until someone has the courage to name the dynamic and break the cycle. Culture doesn't break all at once. It breaks in meetings, one avoided conversation at a time. Start fixing things by naming what's happening. The numbers aren't there. The transition left scars. The perception hasn't caught up to reality. Whatever the thing is, say it out loud. Then solve things together.

Next up: You've fixed the trust, and your meetings are healthy. Great. Now look at your calendar. Seventeen meetings this week, five of them pointless, three overlapping, and you're pretty sure at least half were emails. Let's talk about the tactical nightmare of an overbooked calendar. And how to declare meeting bankruptcy before it declares you.

8

MY CALENDAR, THE REALM OF IMPOSSIBILITY

Your meetings are healthy now. You've got trust. You're solving issues with IDS. People are speaking up. The culture is solid. Great. Now look at your calendar.

Seventeen meetings this week. Five back-to-back days. Three overlaps. Rock time keeps getting booked over. And somewhere around 2 p.m. on Wednesday, you realize you haven't done any work. Just meetings about work.

Welcome to Calendar Jenga.

Time is the only non-renewable resource you have as a leader. You can raise more money. You can hire more people. You can fix a broken culture. But you can't manufacture more hours in the day.

Most leaders hand over their calendars like community property. Anyone can book with you. Anytime. For anything. Saying no feels harder than accepting another hour of your life you'll never get back.

I'm not going to give you time management tips. I want to help you take back control of the one resource you don't waste. Your calendar reflects your priorities. Whether you like those priorities or not.

Look at your calendar, then fix it.

The Game You Don't Win

**ONE MORE MEETING =
EVERYTHING COLLAPSES.**

*"You're always one move away from
everything falling apart."*

I call this Calendar Jenga because that's what this feels like. You're trying to figure out what block to pull out without making the whole thing collapse. You pull something out, you stack this back on top somewhere else. In the endless game, you're always one move from everything falling apart.

Here's what happened to one of our team members earlier this year. Tim covered the CMO role temporarily, and his calendar exploded. Meetings stacked on meetings. No gaps. No breathing room. Straight through, every day, for weeks.

And the work? The work requiring thinking? Pushed to nights. Weekends. The margins.

This is how this happens. Slowly. One accepted invite at a time. Until your calendar owns you.

When Meetings Become the Work

The dangerous part about Calendar Jenga isn't being busy. When your time is overloaded, your brain recalibrates what "creating value" means. You start measuring productivity by how many meetings you got through. Not what you accomplished. Not what you decided. Did I make it through all seventeen without canceling any?

I notice this in myself. On days when I have gaps, like today, I almost don't know what to do with them. I do, but I don't. The value has shifted to getting through all the meetings instead of having two hours to work on content.

Two hours to work on content? Thoughtful work. Deep work. The kind moving the business forward. When your calendar is full, this work becomes an afterthought. Something you squeeze in between meetings or push to Saturday morning.

Here's the thing. If you're a leader modeling this behavior, your team is watching. You're involuntarily teaching them that meetings are the work, being busy equals being valuable, and having a packed calendar means you're important.

None of this is true. Your calendar teaches it anyway.

The EOS Answer: Clarity Breaks

In EOS, we talk about clarity breaks.[23] A clarity break is a scheduled block of time where you step away from the daily grind and think. Not respond to emails. Not put out fires. Not sit in another meeting about the meeting you had yesterday. Think.

You work ON the business instead of IN the business. You ask the questions you never get to during the week. Are we focused on the right things? Is the right person in the right seat? What issue keeps showing up on the list every single week and why haven't we solved the thing? Where are we headed in 90 days, and do I believe we'll get there?

These are the questions running a business demands. And they need silence, space, and your full attention. You won't get to them between back-to-back calls. You won't get to them while you're multitasking through a status update. You get to them when you sit down, close the laptop, and give yourself permission to be a leader instead of a doer for an hour.

Not optional. Scheduled. On your calendar. Protected.

---

[23]   A Clarity Break is a scheduled block of time where leaders step away from day-to-day work to think "on" the business instead of "in" the business. Scheduled weekly, monthly, or at intervals to restore clarity and confidence. Learn more at EOSWorldwide.com.

Why? If you don't schedule them, they won't happen. Your calendar will fill itself. Trust me. Someone will book over the empty Wednesday afternoon. They'll see white space and assume this is available.

People still book over them when you schedule Clarity Breaks. I'll put "Rock Time" on my calendar, and Redmond (our Visionary's executive assistant) will schedule right over top of it. I get this. I do the same thing back to him. Our Visionary has "midday break" on his calendar, and I'm like, "Well, he doesn't need a break. This is the only time five people can meet."

Does our Visionary need the midday break? Yes. Should I respect this? Also yes. Do I? Not always. I'm trying to shoehorn a meeting into an impossible calendar, and his break looks like the best option.

This is the transparency problem. We all see each other's calendars. Sounds great until this becomes an excuse to ignore boundaries. "Well, I see you're free, so…"

Let me give you two examples of what a clarity break looks like when you do the thing right.

I coached a founder in manufacturing. She ran a forty-person company. Her calendar was wall-to-wall Monday through Thursday. Every Friday morning, she blocked 7 a.m. to 10 a.m. as her clarity break. No calls. No Slack. Phone in a drawer. She'd go to a coffee shop three miles from the office so nobody walked in with "a quick question." During one of those Friday sessions, she realized her VP of Operations was the wrong person in the seat. She'd felt it in her gut for months. But she never had the space to sit with the thought long enough to trust her instinct. Two weeks later, she made the change. Her team started hitting their Rocks for the first time in three quarters. She told me, "I made more progress in three hours at a coffee shop than I did in forty hours of meetings the rest of the week."

Another client, an Integrator at a $20 million services company, took a different approach. He blocked ninety minutes every Wednesday after lunch. Stayed in his office. Closed the door. His one rule: no screens for the first thirty minutes. He'd sit with a notebook and write down what was bothering him about the business. Not tasks. Not to-dos. The stuff keeping him up at night. One Wednesday, he wrote down, "We have no succession plan for three of our five department heads." No one had put the issue on the Issues List because the company was growing and things felt good. He brought the thing to the next quarterly. They built a people plan. Twelve months later, one of those department heads left. They had a successor ready. He told me the clarity break saved them six months of chaos.

Two different leaders. Two different approaches. Same result. They gave themselves the space to think, and the thinking changed the business.

Rock time isn't free time. Reading and writing time isn't optional. These are the blocks where you do the work that requires thought. The work that's not happening in meetings.

But in a badge-of-honor culture, where your availability is how you're judged, protecting this time feels rebellious.

The Badge of Honor Problem

We have this culture at Ninety. Maybe you do too. It's subtle, but there.

"We love Fiona because she's always available."

Although it sounds like a compliment, it's not healthy. We say it anyway.

Here's what we're saying. We value responsiveness over boundaries. We value being busy over being effective. We value saying yes over protecting your energy.

Once this is the culture, everyone feels the pressure to maintain availability. Never say no. Never have "Rock Time" people respect. Answer Slack at 11 p.m. because high performers do.

Except they don't. High performers protect their time. They know when they're sharpest, and they guard those hours. They say no to less-important meetings so they can say yes to the work that matters.

A few colleagues and I had a conversation about this. I used to schedule my Slack messages. I'd write them on Saturday afternoon, but schedule them to send Monday morning at 8 a.m. Seemed considerate, right?

My colleague goes, "No, don't do this. People need to know you're working."

I'm like, "This is super freaking disruptive! They're getting Slack messages on Saturday afternoon instead of Monday morning. How is that better?"

The truth is, it isn't better. "Visibility equals value" is badge of honor culture. Even when this is at the expense of everyone's sanity.

The problem compounds when you're remote or hybrid. We've got people on the West Coast. People on the East Coast. One of my clients has specialty roles they had to fill from outside their area, so now they've got team members spread across three time zones.

When do you schedule the meeting? Someone's morning is someone else's afternoon. Someone's end-of-day is someone's lunch. The expectation becomes be flexible. Be available. Make this work.

Translation: sacrifice your boundaries because we haven't figured out a better system.

No boundaries is not sustainable. You end up with leaders working around the clock because someone is always awake and needs something. There's always a meeting you must attend. There's always Slack activity pulling your attention.

The answer isn't to work less. Work smarter. Set boundaries and hold them. Stop treating availability as the primary metric of commitment. But this requires intention. And courage. In most organizations, the person setting boundaries first gets labeled as "not a team player."

That label is garbage, but real.

Energy Management Over Time Management

Most calendar advice ignores energy. You schedule Rock Time at 4 p.m. every day. If your energy is shot by 4 p.m., this time is useless.

For me, Rock Time needs to be in the mornings. I've worked out. I'm caffeinated. Hydrated. Ready to think. By 3 p.m.? Not so much. Yes, more caffeine. But I'm not at the same level of clarity.

Some people are the opposite. Morning meetings are fine for them. They hit their stride after lunch.

The point? Know your energy patterns and schedule accordingly. Put your hardest thinking work in your peak energy windows. Put the meetings that don't require heavy decision-making into your lower energy times.

Don't view this strategy as self-indulgent. It's strategic. You're a better leader, a better thinker, and a better decision-maker when you're working with your energy instead of against it.

Know your energy levels.

Most calendars don't account for this. They stack meetings wherever there's space. And we wonder why we're exhausted.

The FOMO Trap[IP]

Fear of missing out is killing your calendar. Leaders and Visionaries suffer from FOMO. They want to be in every meeting. Know every decision. Hear every discussion. What if something important happens and they're not there?

I'll be honest. I struggle with this. At Vox Mobile, I was everywhere. Every client meeting. Every pitch. Every deal closing.

Then one day, someone on my team said, "You never give us a chance to fail."

Ouch.

They were right. I wasn't scaling the business. I was becoming the bottleneck. Every time something critical came up, I'd jump on another plane and handle it myself. From my perspective, we needed the money, we couldn't miss the quarter, and I knew I could get it done, so I did.

But here's what I didn't see. The next generation couldn't learn. They never got to try, fail, adjust, and try again. They never got to build the skills they needed because I kept jumping in.

FOMO looks like leadership and feels like ownership, but it's fear. Fear that without you, this won't work. Fear that if you're not there, something will break. This fear will fill your calendar until there's nothing left.

> **FOMO looks like leadership and feels like ownership, but it's fear.**

Here's the truth. If your business doesn't function without you in every meeting, you haven't built a business. You've built a job. A job burning you out.

The Vicious Cycle

FEAR:
"Without me, it won't work."

BEHAVIOR:
Attend every meeting

RESULT:
Calendar completely full

FEAR CONFIRMED:
"See? They need me!"

CONSEQUENCE:
No time to work ON business

BREAK THE CYCLE:

If your business can't function
without you in every meeting,
you've haven't built a business.
You've built a job."

The transition from Visionary-in-every-meeting to leader-who-empowers-the-team is hard. Requires trust. Requires letting go. Requires accepting sometimes people will make decisions differently than you would have. Sometimes they'll make mistakes. This is how they learn. This is how your business scales. This is how you get your calendar and your life back.

The question isn't "Should I miss this meeting?" The question is, "Should I keep showing up to every meeting like this for the next five years?" If the answer is no, start building the systems and the team functioning without you in the room.

The solution starts with your calendar. Stop accepting every invitation. Start declining meetings where you're not essential. Empower your team to make decisions and cascade the information to you afterward.

Will you miss some things? Yes. Will some decisions be wrong? Also yes. This is the cost of scaling. Cheaper than burning out or becoming the reason your business doesn't grow.

The Cascading Message Problem

Another calendar trap is the "I need to be there so I know what's happening" problem. Our Visionary doesn't need to be in the go-to-market meeting. He thinks he does. How else will he know what was decided? This is a "cascading information" issue, rather than a "he needs to be there" issue.

The information decided upon needs to make its way to the Visionary, but that's Laura's job, Candace's job, or Peter's job. They're in the meeting. They know what was decided. They cascade this message to our Visionary.

At Ninety, we don't do this nearly enough. We talk about this. We know we should. We don't build this into the rhythm.

At the end of every issue you solve using IDS, you're supposed to ask, "Who else needs to know about this decision?" If somebody not in the room needs to know, you cascade it. Right then. Add this to their team's headlines. Send a message. Make the information flow.

We have the technology to do this, but we don't. So instead, leaders fill their calendars trying to be in every meeting where decisions might happen.

Not leadership. Poor information architecture.

Decision Rights: The Missing Piece

If your company is struggling with the Cascading Message Problem, you need clarity on decision rights.

In your seat, what decisions do you make? What decisions require input from someone else? What decisions need to be escalated?

Most teams don't have this clarity. People make decisions they don't have the authority to make. Or worse, they don't make decisions because they're not sure what is their decision to make.

What happens? More meetings. To clarify. To discuss. To loop people in who should have been looped in earlier.

We end up in other IDS sessions because somebody made a decision they didn't have the right to make. They assumed they had the authority. They didn't know what rights they had. Now we've got a problem to untangle.

If we had clarity on decision rights built into the Accountability Chart, visible in the tool, and agreed upon by the team, half of these meetings wouldn't need to happen.

IN YOUR SEAT, WHAT DECISIONS DO YOU MAKE ?

DECISION TYPE	YOUR AUTHORITY	REQUIRES INPUT	MUST ESCALATE
Daily execution	✔ You decide		
Budget < $5K	✔ You decide.	Inform finance	
Hiring for team	Consult	With HR/leader	
Budget > $25K	—	—	Finance / leader
Strategy shift	—	—	Leadership team
Visionary decides	—	—	Visionary decides

Clear decision rights = Fewer meetings

People make decisions they don't have authority to make...

...More meetings to untangle.

People would know which decisions are theirs to make, which the Visionary needs to make, or which one requires final approval from the Head of Customer Support.

Your calendar will breathe a sigh of relief.

The Calendar Audit

How do you fix this?

Audit your calendar. Hold up each recurring meeting and ask, "Does this drive results?"

If the answer is no, it has got to go.

Here's how.

Step 1: Audit your recurring meetings.

Pull up your calendar. Look at everything repeating. Weekly one-on-ones. Team syncs. Status updates. All of this.

Write them down. Put them in a spreadsheet if this helps. See the full picture.

Count how many hours per week you're spending in recurring meetings. I'm guessing more than you think. For most leaders, it's 15-25 hours. More than half your work week gone before you've done a single hour of work.

Step 2: Ask the hard questions.

For each meeting, ask:

- What's the purpose of this meeting?
- Is this purpose being achieved?
- Could this information be shared another way?
- Does everyone invited need to be there?
- If we canceled this meeting, what would break?

Be honest. Most meetings fail at least one of these questions.

The "weekly touch base with the team"? What's this accomplishing? Solving issues or giving status updates? Status updates could be an async Slack message or a headline in your Level 10 Meeting.

The "quick sync" that has been on your calendar for the past six months? When's the last time this was quick? Or useful? If it could be canceled or rescheduled, maybe it wasn't as essential as you thought.

Test it. Pick one recurring meeting and cancel it for two weeks. See what breaks. If nothing breaks, you don't need the meeting. If something breaks, you've identified what the meeting should be about. Redesign to focus on this.

Step 3: Kill, compress, or convert.

Kill. Cancel meetings when they don't serve a clear purpose. No guilt. Delete them. If someone needs the meeting, they'll ask for it back. When they do, make them articulate why this is essential.

Compress. Shorten meetings when they regularly end early. If your one-hour meeting wraps in 30 minutes, make it a 30-minute meeting. Meetings expand to fill the time allotted. Give them less time and watch what happens. People get more focused, more efficient.

Convert. Turn status update meetings into async updates. Use Slack. Use headlines in your Level 10 Meeting. Stop gathering six people for information that could've been a paragraph.

I worked with a client who had a weekly "all-hands standup" taking an hour. Fifteen people. Every Monday. Going around the room with updates.

We killed this. Replaced this with a Slack channel where people posted their weekly updates every Monday morning. Three bullet points. Done.

The team got their hour back. The information still flowed. The people who needed to sync on something scheduled targeted time to do so. Fifteen hours of collective time saved. Every week. Nearly two full-time employees' worth of capacity, by killing one pointless meeting.

Step 4: Protect your Rock Time.

Schedule and label this clearly. "Rock Time - Do Not Book." Make it recurring. Put it in your peak energy windows.

Then defend the time. When someone tries to book over it, push back. "I've got Rock Time then. Can we do this another time instead?" If it's urgent, fine. Move your Rock Time. Most things aren't. Most things can wait twenty-four hours.

You might feel guilty at first. Like you're being difficult. Here's the thing. You can't lead effectively if you never have time to think. You can't solve strategic problems if you're always in tactical meetings. You can't work ON the business if you're always IN meetings about the business.

Protecting your Rock Time isn't selfish. It's necessary.

Step 5: Build in buffer.

Stop stacking meetings back-to-back. Give yourself fifteen minutes between calls. Use this to decompress. To take notes. To think about what happened before you jump into the next thing.

Your brain needs transition time. Your calendar should reflect this.

I know what you're thinking. "I don't have fifteen minutes between meetings. My calendar is too packed."

This is the problem. Your calendar is too packed because you've accepted every meeting request coming your way. Now you're playing Calendar Jenga every week, trying to make this all fit.

Buffer time forces you to be more selective. You don't say yes to everything if you're building in transition time. You have to prioritize. You have to say no to meetings if they don't matter.

Step 6: Practice the cascade.

At the end of every Level 10 Meeting, ask, "Who else needs to know what we decided today?"

Write down the answer. Assign someone to cascade the information. Put it in headlines. Send it to the relevant team.

Build the cascade into your meeting rhythm. Make this part of the closing process. Don't end the meeting until you've identified what needs to cascade and to whom.

Information should flow without requiring everyone to be in every meeting. It won't flow automatically. You have to build the systems to make this happen.

At Ninety, we have the technology to cascade messages. As I mentioned before, we don't use this consistently enough, but it's something we're working to fix.

Every message cascading properly is one less meeting someone has to attend "to stay informed."

AUDIT RECURRING MEETINGS	**ASK HARD QUESTIONS**	**KILL, COMPRESS, OR CONVERT**
☐ List everything that repeats ☐ Count weekly hours (15-25? More than half your week?)	☐ What's the purpose? ☐ Is it still being achieved? ☐ Could this be async? ☐ What breaks if we cancel?	☐ Kill: No clear purpose ☐ Compress: Ends early? Make it shorter ☐ Convert: Status updates → async
1	2	3
PROTECT ROCK TIME	**BUILD IN BUFFER**	**PRACTICE THE CASCADE**
☐ Schedule in peak energy times ☐ Label clearly: "Do Not Book" ☐ Defend it	☐ 15 minutes between meetings ☐ Decompress, think, transition	☐ "Who else needs to know?" ☐ Assign cascade responsibility ☐ Build into meeting rhythm
4	5	6

Meeting Bankruptcy: The Nuclear Option

Sometimes your calendar is so broken incremental fixes won't work. You need to declare meeting bankruptcy. Here's how. Cancel everything. Yes, everything. All recurring meetings. Wipe the slate.

Rebuild from scratch. Start with the EOS rhythms:

- Level 10 Meeting with your leadership team
- Level 10 Meeting with your direct reports
- Quarterly Conversations
- Quarterly Planning sessions
- Annual Planning

Add only what's essential. If that feels extreme, you're right; it is extreme. Sometimes this is what it takes to break the cycle.

One of my clients did this last year. The calendar was chaos. Overlapping meetings. No focus time. Constant firefighting. The leadership team was burned out. Decisions were slow. Issues weren't getting solved because nobody had time to think.

We looked at the calendar during a quarterly session. I asked, "How much time do you spend in meetings each week?"

The Visionary did the math. "About thirty-five hours."

I said, "More than a full-time job. When do you run the company?"

Silence.

We declared meeting bankruptcy. Canceled everything for two weeks. Rebuilt with intention.

The first week was uncomfortable. People didn't know what to do with all the space. They felt guilty for not being in meetings. Like they weren't working hard enough.

By week two, things started clicking. Issues that had been stuck for months got solved because people had time to think. Languishing Rocks moved forward. The team started communicating differently. More directly, less performatively.

They rebuilt the calendar with only the essential meetings. L10s. Quarterly planning. A few critical client check-ins. Done.

The result? They went from thirty-five hours of meetings per week to fifteen. The business didn't fall apart. In fact, everything got better. Faster decisions. Clearer communication. Less burnout.

Not everyone needs to go nuclear. But if your calendar is choking your business, this is an option.

Here's the thing about declaring bankruptcy. It sends a message to the team and to yourself that your time matters. Meetings aren't sacred. You're willing to blow up the status quo to fix what's broken.

The Real Cost of a Bad Calendar

Let's talk about what an overbooked calendar costs you.

First, the obvious. Your time. If you're spending 25 hours a week in meetings, this is 1,300 hours a year. More than 32 full work weeks. You've spent more than half your year in meetings.

The real cost isn't time. It's the opportunity cost.

What could you have done with those 1,300 hours? What strategic initiatives could you have driven? What customer relationships could you have deepened? What problems could you have solved?

Instead, you sat in meetings. Many didn't matter. Some made things worse.

There's also the cost to your team. When you're always in meetings, you're not available for the conversations that matter. The quick check-in preventing a crisis. The coaching moment unlocking someone's potential. The decision waiting for your input for three days because your calendar has no gaps.

Your team will learn to work around you if they have to. They either make decisions without you (and sometimes get this wrong), or they delay decisions until they get on your calendar (and lose momentum). Neither is good.

Then there's the cost to your health. Mental. Physical. Emotional.

You don't sustain thirty-five hours of meetings per week without burning out. Your brain needs downtime. Your body needs movement. Your relationships need attention.

25 hours/week x **52** weeks = **1,300** hours/year =
32 full workweeks = more than **HALF** your year

OPPORTUNITY COST: What could you have done with **1,300** hours?

→ Strategic incentives not driven
→ Customer relationships not deepened
→ Problems not solved
→ Team members not coached

You didn't spend the time. **You traded it for meetings.**

When your calendar is packed, those things become optional. You skip lunch. You cancel the gym. You miss dinner with your family because there's one more call.

This behavior is not sustainable, not noble, and is bad leadership.

A good leader protects their calendar so they show up fully for the things that matter. A bad leader lets their calendar run them until they've got nothing left to give.

Before we wrap this chapter, remember that your calendar is not neutral. It either works for you or against you. If you're drowning in meetings, this is working against you.

Fix this by:

- Scheduling clarity breaks and protecting them
- Understanding your energy patterns and scheduling accordingly
- Letting go of FOMO and trusting your team to handle decisions
- Building cascading messages into your meeting rhythm
- Clarifying decision rights so people know what's theirs to decide

- Audit your recurring meetings
- Declaring meeting bankruptcy if you need a reset

Your calendar should serve your priorities. Not the other way around.

"Meetings Suck Less" Realization

Calendar Jenga isn't a game you win. It's one you stop playing. Every meeting you accept is a trade. Your time and energy for whatever value this meeting creates. Most meetings are bad trades. They don't create enough value to justify the cost. Stop accepting them. Schedule clarity breaks and defend them like your business depends on this. Because this does. Leaders who don't protect their own calendars don't lead effectively. Simple as that.

Up Next: You've cleaned up your calendar. Now let's talk about which meetings deserve to be there, and which ones you think are special but aren't.

YOUR MEETING IS NOT SPECIAL

Look, I get it. You think your meeting is different. Your team is different. Your industry is different. The issues you're dealing with are way more complex than what some operating system can handle.

Spoiler: They're not.

I've spent two decades building companies and coaching leadership teams. I've sat through meetings in tech, manufacturing, healthcare, professional services. I've been in rooms with three people and rooms with thirty. Here's what I've learned: 99 percent of the time, your meeting isn't as special as you think.

Most meetings fall into predictable categories. And most of them suck for predictable reasons. The good news? Once you understand the patterns, you can fix them. Fast.

This chapter breaks down the most common meeting types. What works and what doesn't. How to run each one so you don't feel like you're dying by PowerPoint.

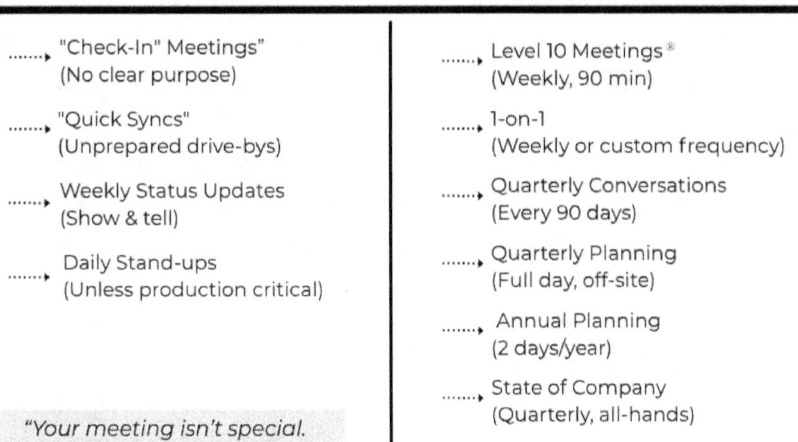

The Meetings You're Already Having (And Probably Hating)

The "Check-In Meeting"

We've done this at Ninety, so I'm not calling anyone out here. I'm owning up to patterns we all fall into.

Check-in meetings are terrible meetings. Someone throws one on your calendar. "Hey, we need to check in." But here's the problem: what's the purpose of a check-in? All great meetings have a defined objective and an agenda supporting the objective. They also need a conclusion. But if we're checking in with each other, what's the point?

People will say, "Well, I want to be on the same page." Okay. Do this async through Slack. Use Ninety. Share information through a Scorecard. If there's something real to talk about, make an issue and bring the issue to your Issues List.

"See, issue, solve." If you see something, put the thing in an issue somewhere so you do something about it. Then solve the thing. But if we don't have something to solve, and I'm not going to create an issue, then you and I are going to catch up? There's some need for human connectivity there, sure. We're all human. But otherwise, what are we doing with our time?

You start to see check-in meetings littering calendars. And one-on-ones often become, "Oh, John and I have a one-on-one every week." Okay. What are we doing? If we're issuing things and solving things, great. But otherwise? Not productive.

So how do you know if your check-ins have crossed the line from helpful to habit? Simple. You run the Calendar Audit.

There are some situations where these meetings start with great intentions. Maybe somebody's new, like when Kate joined our marketing team seven or eight months ago. I had a one-on-one with Kate for the first few months, making sure I was available for her and anything she needed. But then I dropped the meeting the next quarter. We have other meetings together. If she finds herself in a place where she needs something from me, we'll throw the thing on the calendar. But a standing meeting? Doesn't make sense.

Some of those patterns people get started with have great intentions. Maybe somebody is new; maybe there was a challenge. And you keep the meeting almost by happenstance.

When a senior leader has check-ins or one-on-ones with people in other areas because they're trying to develop rhythm or mentorship, it can be a wonderful practice. But if they go on for a long time, you need to know: Is this healthy? Does this make sense? We've seen those patterns in our organization, and we always pause to check whether there is actually mentorship happening. If not, we have too much to do as an organization to let those meetings continue.

And we all know Zoom and Teams are fatiguing at some point. When you're on them back-to-back-to-back all day long, you're not productive.

Speaking of unproductive meetings eating up your day, let me introduce you to the worst offender of all.

The "Quick Sync"

Let's start with everyone's favorite lie: the quick sync.

You know the one. Someone throws "A quick sync, fifteen minutes max," on your calendar. Except the thing is never only fifteen minutes. The meeting runs for forty-five minutes, and half of the time is spent figuring out why you're even on the call.

I had a VP once who scheduled seventeen quick syncs in a single week. Seventeen. When I asked him why, he said, "I need to quickly align with everyone." Translation: "I haven't thought through what I need, so I'm going to think out loud on everyone else's time."

Quick syncs exist because someone didn't prepare.

Quick syncs exist because someone didn't prepare. They didn't write down the issue. They didn't think through what they need. So instead, they drag you into a conversation better suited for a Slack message.

Here's the fix: kill them. Seriously. If the issue is important enough to pull someone away from their work, the issue is important enough to prepare for. Put the thing on the Issues List. Bring it to your Level 10 Meeting. Stop treating other people's time like the resource is free.

The only exception is a true emergency. But if everything is an emergency, nothing is.

One client I worked with was drowning in quick syncs. We did an audit. Turns out, 80 percent of them could be handled asynchronously. The other 20 percent? Those were real issues deserving proper IDS time, not a drive-by conversation.

CLIENT AUDIT: 17 "QUICK SYNCS" IN ONE WEEK

Results:

80% could be handled async
→ Slack message
→ Email
→ Add to Issues List

20% were real issues
→ Needed proper IDS®time
→ Not drive-by conversations

The Fix:

If you need **face time**, write down the issue **first**
→ Context
→ Impact
→ What decision needs to be made?

RESULT: HALF THE **"URGENT"** MEETINGS DISAPPEARED
(Because writing it down = realized not urgent or already knew the answer)

We killed the quick syncs and added a rule: If you need face time, you write down the issue first, including the context, the impact, and what decision needs to be made. Suddenly, half the "urgent" meetings disappeared. Because when you have to write the thing down, you realize it is either not urgent or you already know the answer.

Now, quick syncs are bad because they waste time without structure. But at least they're short. Want to know what's worse? When you formalize the time-wasting into a recurring calendar invite.

Show-and-Tell Meetings

These are the weekly check-in meetings where everyone goes around the room and gives updates. Sales gives their update. Marketing gives theirs. Operations gives theirs. Everyone nods politely. Nothing gets solved.

I call these Show-and-Tell meetings. Remember elementary school? You'd bring your toy dinosaur, tell everyone about the thing, and then sit down. These meetings feel like you're back in elementary school. Except now you're all getting paid six figures to show and tell your way through an hour.

If you're running a meeting where the primary activity is listening to people report out, you're doing it wrong. Updates belong in a dashboard, a Scorecard, or an email. Meetings are for solving problems.

When I work with teams stuck in this pattern, I ask one question: "What would happen if we canceled this meeting?" Nine times out of ten, they admit nothing would change. Because the meeting isn't driving any decisions.

Here's what one of my clients told me: "We have a weekly leadership meeting. Everyone reports their numbers. Everyone says they're 'on track' or 'working on the thing.' We nod. We adjourn. Then we go back to our desks and wonder why nothing ever changes."

Sound familiar?

The shift is simple but hard: Move updates to pre-work. Use a shared Scorecard everyone sees before the meeting. Then spend the meeting time on IDS. Identify, Discuss, Solve. Isolate the valuable part.

When you make this switch, you'll get pushback. People are comfortable with show-and-tell. It feels productive. Feels safe. Nobody has to make a hard decision or have a tough conversation.

But comfortable doesn't build companies. Solving issues does.

And you know what's even more comfortable than a weekly show-and-tell? Doing the thing every single day. Enter the stand-up meeting.

The Standing "Stand-Up"

Enter Isabelle, the Head of Sales. When I first started working with her company on their EOS implementation, I said, "Hey, every department can have a Level 10 Meeting. They're a little different depending on the size, but the structure exists."

And Isabelle said, "No, I don't need this. I meet with all my salespeople all the time." She had five or six salespeople.

I asked her, "Do you think the patterns repeat?"

"What do you mean?"

"Do they repeat? Like, one person's issue is another person's issue. They learn from the thing."

"Yeah, I know they mention this. The patterns are similar."

"So what if they were all in the room when the thing happened? What if they all heard the other person's repeat pattern problem, and you solved the thing one time, versus five or six?"

She didn't like the answer at first. But she said, "Okay, I'll try this for a quarter and let you know."

She did. And she came back the next quarter and said, "This was phenomenal. I had one meeting for 90 minutes a week, instead of five or six meetings."

This was the pattern she was used to. As the company grew, she maintained the same behavior as she scaled from one salesperson to the five or six they had when I began working with them. We introduced the Level 10 Meeting and said, "Trust this for a quarter. Give me a quarter. If it doesn't work, let's talk about it then." But it worked.

We see this pattern a lot with stand-up meetings. We've even done this at Ninety when we were smaller. Lots of stand-ups. Then you inspect them, and you're like, "This is people relating. Checking in." Eight people for twenty minutes a day in the morning. What the heck are we doing?

If you still want to do this, hold the stand-up on Wednesdays only. Or Fridays. But don't do it every day. Those are early patterns you keep carrying as you grow.

This issue is what I call a Legacy Hangover[IP]. "This is the way we've done the thing, and it is sort of working, so we're gonna keep doing things this way."

PHASE 1:
MEETING STARTS WITH
GOOD REASON
(Crisis, new person, specific problem)

PHASE 2:
REASON SOLVED, BUT
MEETING CONTINUES
"This is sort of working, so..."

PHASE 3:
2 YEARS LATER,
STILL MEETING
"This is the way we've done it."

PHASE 4:
AUDIT REVEALS:
8 people x 20 minutes/day
= 13 Hours/Week on...what exactly?

DECISION:
KILL IT or REDESIGN IT

"**Legacy hangover**: Carrying patterns past their usefulness because we forgot to audit."

Sometimes, leaders find their value in holding on to legacy habits. They think, "Oh no, what would happen if I didn't do this?" Well, you'd grow again. Leading a meeting is not a leader's value, in my opinion. Something you need to do, sure. But don't view it as where value lives.

A lot of leaders define their success based on how many meetings they have, rather than the quality of a few meetings and their impact in those meetings.

Alright, I've beaten up enough on the meetings, wasting your time. Check-ins, quick syncs, show-and-tell sessions, daily stand-ups. They all share the same fatal flaw: They consume energy without creating value.

So what's the alternative? Let's talk about meetings that work. The ones solving problems, driving decisions, and moving your business forward. These aren't nice to have. If you want to scale, they're foundational.

The Meetings You Should Be Having

Level 10 Meetings

I've said this before, and I'll say this again: the L10 is the heartbeat of your business. It's a weekly, 90-minute meeting with your leadership team (or any team, doesn't matter) following the same agenda every single time.

Why does this work? Structure. Discipline. Accountability.

You walk in knowing exactly what's going to happen:

- Segue (5 min): Good news, personal and professional. Gets everyone present.

- Scorecard review (5 min): Are we on or off track? No storytelling. Data only.

- Rock review (5 min): Are your 90-day priorities moving forward?

- Customer/employee headlines (5 min): Quick wins or issues needing visibility.

- To-do list (5 min): Did everyone do what they said they'd do last week?

- IDS (60 min): This is where the magic happens. Identify the most important issues. Discuss them. Solve them. For real.

- Conclude (5 min): Recap to-dos, rate the meeting, and get out.

The rating is critical. And I love to rate everything. At the end of every Level 10 Meeting, everyone scores from 1 to 10. This habit keeps you honest. If your meetings are consistently below an 8, something's broken.

I've seen teams transform in 90 days by implementing this one format. Suddenly, decisions get made. Problems get solved. People stop feeling like meetings are a waste of time.

Let me tell you about a skeptical team. The Visionary said, "Kris, we've tried structured meetings before. They never stick. People hate them."

I said, "Try this for 90 days. Rate the thing every week. If it's not working, we'll change it."

Week one: They rated the thing a 6. It was too rigid and felt forced. Fair enough.

Week three: Rated a 7. Starting to see the value. Issues were getting solved.

Week eight: Rated a 9. The Visionary pulled me aside and said, "I don't believe I'm saying this, but people are asking when the next Level 10 Meeting is. They want to bring issues to the meeting instead of trying to solve everything in hallway conversations."

By the twelfth week, they couldn't imagine running the business without it.

Here's why this works: predictability creates trust. When everyone knows the format, knows their role, knows what to expect, they come prepared. They bring the real issues. They engage.

And those 60 minutes of IDS is where your business gets run. Not in email threads. Not in Slack channels. Not in drive-by conversations. In a focused hour where you identify what matters most, discuss the thing openly, and solve the thing permanently.

One more thing: the Level 10 Meeting only works if you do the thing every week. Same day. Same time. Non-negotiable. The moment you start skipping weeks or rescheduling, you've told your team the meeting isn't important. And guess what? They'll treat it accordingly.

The L10 handles your team rhythm. But you also need individual connection. This is where one-on-ones come in. And most people get them completely wrong.

One-on-Ones

Here's where most managers blow this: they either skip one-on-ones entirely or they turn them into status updates.

A great one-on-one isn't a check-in. It's a coaching session. Development time. Where you connect with the human being sitting across from you.

Come prepared. Bring your Issues List. Ask questions.

GREAT 1-on-1

- ✓ Coaching session
- ✓ Development time
- ✓ Human connection
- ✓ Ask the questions, then **LISTEN**:
    - *What's working?*
    - *What's not working?*
    - *Where are you stuck?*
    - *How do I help?*
- ✓ Use silence as a tool
- ✓ 30 minutes, non-negotiable

BLOWN 1-on-1

- ✗ Status update session
- ✗ Manager talks the entire time
- ✗ Check boxes, move on
- ✗ Skip when "too busy"
- ✗ Interrupt with solutions
- ✗ Miss early warning signs

And then, listen. Don't interrupt. Don't problem-solve unless they ask for help. Listen.

When I was building VOX Mobile, I had one-on-ones with my direct reports every week. Thirty minutes. Non-negotiable. And I learned more about what was happening in the business from those conversations than from any dashboard or report.

One time, a team member came in and said everything was fine. But I could tell something was off. So I waited. Silence is a tool. After about thirty seconds, she said, "I'm frustrated with how product decisions are getting made. I feel like my input doesn't matter."

One conversation led us to redesign how we involved the engineering team in product planning. If I hadn't made space for it, she would have kept frustration bottled up. And eventually, she would have left.

If you're skipping one-on-ones because you're "too busy," you're making a mistake. You're trading short-term efficiency for long-term effectiveness. And you're missing the early warning signs someone's about to quit or burn out.

Weekly one-on-ones keep the daily connection strong. But every 90 days, you need to zoom out and have a bigger conversation.

Quarterly Conversations

This is one of my favorite tools in EOS. The informal conversation between manager and their direct report is far more valuable than a performance review or a report card. When you're holding these two-way discussions about what's working every ninety days, nothing feels like a surprise. If there's an issue, you're catching the thing in week 8, not week 48. And if someone's crushing it, they hear about it in real time, not six months later in some formal review.

Here's the part most people miss: feedback goes both ways. Your direct report gets to tell you what's working and what's not about your leadership, so you get a chance for real growth as well.

We built this into Ninety because I got tired of dreading annual reviews. Quarterly Conversations are lighter, more frequent, and way more useful. If you're not doing them, start.

Those Quarterly Conversations happen one-on-one. But your leadership team also needs to come together every 90 days to recalibrate.

Quarterly Planning Sessions

Every 90 days, your leadership team needs to step out of the day-to-day grind and look ahead. Your Quarterly Planning session.

This is where you:

- Review last quarter's results (revenue, profit, Rocks, Scorecard).
- Refresh your Vision/Traction Organizer. Make sure everyone's still aligned on where you're going.
- Set next quarter's Rocks. What are the 3-7 priorities moving the business forward?
- Solve the biggest issues blocking your path.

This will be an all-day session. Take it off-site if you can swing it. Because if you stay in the office, someone's going to get pulled into a "quick fire drill," and the whole thing falls apart.

The discipline of preparation is required. But if you follow the process and show up with discipline, then you're going to be fine.

What wastes time in these sessions? I still experience this to this day, as much as I try to get clients to follow the structure. We do "quarter in review". Great check-in. Then Scorecard review: lagging indicators, leading indicators, and Rocks. Rocks are not the hard part.

The hard part is when people show up unprepared. They haven't reviewed the numbers. They haven't thought through what worked and what didn't. And now we're spending the first hour of an all-day session catching everyone up on things they should have done as pre-work.

I've led hundreds of these sessions. The teams doing them religiously? They grow faster. They solve problems proactively. They don't get blindsided by issues festering for months.

The teams skipping them? They drift. Priorities get fuzzy. People start working on different agendas. And before you know this, you're wondering why nothing's getting done.

Quarterly Planning gives you the 90-day pulse. But once a year, you need to go even bigger.

Annual Planning Sessions

Once a year, you need to zoom all the way out for your Annual Planning session.

This is a two-day event. Day one is strategy. Day two is your regular Quarterly Planning session, but with more context.

On day one, you're asking big questions:

- Are our Core Values still right?
- Is our Core Focus still clear?
- Are we still on track for our 10-Year Target?
- What needs to change in our Three-Year Picture?
- What's our one-year plan?

Nothing is sacred. Everything is on the table. You want debate. You want tension. Because this is where you make sure the leadership team is aligned. Not just saying the words, but seeing the same future.

All these meetings (weekly, quarterly, annual) are for your leadership team. But you don't forget about everyone else in the company. They need to know what's happening too.

State of the Company Meetings

Here's a meeting type that often doesn't get enough love: the all-hands, State of the Company meeting.

This is where you bring everyone together. The whole company. And you tell them what's happening. Where we are. Where we're going. What's working. What's not.

Transparency builds trust. And trust builds culture.

Most companies hold a State of the Company meeting quarterly. The frequency matters less than the consistency. But here's where most companies blow this: they treat State of the Company as something to get through versus something to grow through.

The "Get Through It" Problem

Leaders are checking the box. "We did a great State of the Company. We delivered the thing." But was the thing engaging? Did you get feedback? Did people walk away energized, or did they walk away feeling like they sat through another presentation?

I always tell my clients: put your Core Value shout-outs as close to the front as you can possibly get them. Because shout-outs generate engagement and positivity. People are excited to celebrate each other. When you bury shout-outs at the back of the meeting, people are done by the time you get there. You lose the whole thing.

So bring celebration to the front for engagement, versus bearing the thing at the back where people are already checking out. State of the Companies go off the rails, maybe. But most of the time, people are phoning it in and checking the box versus creating engagement.

The Q&A Disaster

Q&As are rough. If you don't get some Issues ahead of time, you get crickets. Companies doing this well harvest questions ahead of time. That way, you have three to five things already on the Issues list to get started.

These are things the leaders have surfaced or have gone and asked their teams. "Hey, State of the Company's coming up. Give us three to five things on your mind to talk about."

Then it opens the door. Otherwise, you see the tyranny of the blank page, and everyone is silent. They don't say anything. And then we're like, "Oh, I guess we've got no Issues." Well, we know that isn't true. Let's do this differently.

Stop Reading Financials

It's easy to fall into a readout of financials as a standard practice, but I encourage clients not to do this. Instead, provide them ahead of time. We recently had to have Part 2 of our State of the Company meeting after Part 1 because we ran out of time due to reading financials. Come on. If they don't take the time to read the thing, then that's on them. Give the financials to them ahead of time. Let's not read out financials on the call.

If you want to provide a summary, sure. But make more time to discuss. If they have questions on the financials, we'll talk about those. But otherwise, we're going through the metrics and going, "Oh, this is what this did, and this is what happened."

Waste of time.

Who Should Speak?

The Visionary should not be the one to talk the whole time. Like in any good meeting, someone must be the facilitator, and someone must be the Note Taker.

This last time at Ninety, I was determined to make the thing punchy and fun enough to keep people from staring blankly at the screen. Aiming to facilitate engagement.

It's an important part someone needs to play. Be engaging, pull the team in as much as possible through banter, stories, or whatever your thing is. Get everyone involved. I don't think there's a seat defining this. But if there's somebody inside the company who wants to do it, who has the skills to do it, they should go for it. Don't always put this on the Visionary or CFO. Don't always pick the Chief Funny Guy or whatever.

Treat it more as a job for whoever has the skills and the desire to do it, versus thinking, "Oh, I'm the Visionary, I have to do this." Maybe the Visionary's commentary is here and there and is much better than them thinking they have to navigate the whole thing.

What Makes a Meeting "Special" (Hint: Not What You Think)

You want your meetings to be special? Stop trying to be special. Follow the format. Do the work. Show up prepared. Make decisions. Solve problems. Hold people accountable.

The magic isn't in the agenda. Discipline creates the magic when you show up week after week, quarter after quarter, and do the hard work of running the business well.

I've watched teams turn meetings from their most dreaded hour into their most valuable. Not because they found some secret hack. But because they committed to a working system.

EOS gives you this system. The Level 10 Meeting gives you weekly Traction. Quarterly Planning keeps you aligned. Annual Planning keeps you focused on the big picture. One-on-ones keep you connected to your people. None of this is complicated. But all of it requires discipline.

WEEKLY	**QUARTERLY**	**ANNUALLY**
L10® Every week, 90 minutes	**QC: Converations** Every 90 days	**APM: Planning** 2 days, once per year
1-ON-1 Based on person's needs	**QPM: Planning** Full day, off-site	
	SotC: State of Company All-hands	

"The **magic** isn't in the agenda. It's in the **DISCIPLINE** of showing up week after week, quarter after quarter."

Before we wrap this chapter, let's be honest: You're not going to fix all your meetings overnight. Change takes time. Takes buy-in. Takes repetition.

But start small. Pick one meeting type. Try the format. Rate the thing. Adjust. And do the thing again next week.

Over time, those small changes compound. Your meetings get sharper. Your team gets more aligned. Decisions happen faster. Problems get solved instead of lingering.

And before you know this, meetings stop being the thing everyone dreads and start being the thing making everything else work.

"Meetings Suck Less" Realization

Your meeting isn't special. Your meeting type isn't new. The problems you're solving aren't unprecedented. And this is good news. Because this means someone's already figured out how to fix it. Stop reinventing the wheel. Follow a format that works. Show up prepared. Make decisions. Hold people accountable. That's how meetings go from sucking to being the most valuable hours of your week.

Next up: Not every company needs every meeting. The meetings you need depend on where you are right now. Let's talk about meeting your company where the company is.

10

MEETING YOUR COMPANY WHERE IT IS

Not every company needs every meeting. I see this all the time. An early-stage startup tries to run Level 10 Meetings with three people and wonders why the thing feels like overkill. Or a well-established company is still operating like a scrappy garage band, wondering why nothing scales.

The meetings you need depend on where your company is right now. Not where you want to be. Not where you were. Where you are. Let me break this down.

The Five Stages of Development[IP]

Companies grow through predictable stages. And each stage needs a different relationship with time, with structure, and with meetings.

Your time horizon changes as you grow. Early on, you're living day to day. Later, you're thinking in quarters, then years, then decades. The meetings you run need to match where you are.

Stage 1: Start (Day to Day)

You're in survival mode, proving there's something worth building. In this stage, you react to what's in front of you, solve urgent problems, and live day-to-day.

What meetings you need:

One-on-Ones (as needed): When someone's struggling, or you need to course-correct.

What you don't need:

Daily Huddles: You're three people. You're talking all day already.

Level 10 Meetings: Too formal. Too structured. You're three people. You don't need an hour-long meeting with a full agenda.

Quarterly Planning: You're still figuring out if this works. Quarterlies come later.

Annual Planning: You're trying to survive the month.

The trap: Trying to run meetings for a Stage 3 company when you're in Stage 1. This slows you down. Stay lean. Stay fast. Add structure when you earn it.

Stage 2: Build (Week-to-Week)

You've proven something works. Now you're testing assumptions, learning from feedback, seeking product-market fit. You're thinking week-to-week.

What meetings you need:

One-on-Ones: Regular now. Weekly or bi-weekly. You're building a team. You need to know where people are.

What you don't need yet:

Level 10 Meetings: Close, but not quite. You're not ready for the full 90-minute format. You don't have Rocks yet. You're still figuring out your Scorecard.

Quarterly Planning: Getting closer. But you're still in learning mode.

Annual Planning: Too early. You're thinking week-to-week, not year-to-year.

When to add the next level:

When your one-on-ones start feeling chaotic. When the same issues keep coming back. When you realize you need more structure to keep everyone aligned.

This is the moment. Time to move to Level 10 Meetings.

Stage 3: Grow (Month-to-Month, Quarter-to-Quarter)

You're designing processes. Building repeatable patterns. Solidifying your culture. You're no longer reacting. You're building a business to run without constant reinvention. You're thinking in months and quarters.

What meetings you need:

Level 10 Meetings: Now. This is the stage where Level 10 becomes essential. Weekly rhythm. Full structure. Scorecard. Rocks. Issues List. IDS. Conclude. The works.

Quarterly Planning: Time to add these. Pull the team together every 90 days. Review Rocks. Set new ones. Look at what's coming. Build alignment.

One-on-Ones: Regular cadence. Weekly or bi-weekly. You're developing people now.

Quarterly Conversations: No agenda. Trust-based. It's not about what people are working on. These conversations are about how they're doing. How are you feeling about your role? Where do you want to grow? What's getting in your way? This is where you build connection and make sure people feel seen.

What you don't need yet:

Annual Planning: You're thinking quarters, not years. Annuals come at Stage 4.

The trap: Running Level 10 Meetings but skipping Quarterlies. You need both. The weekly keeps you executing. The quarterly keeps you aligned on the bigger picture.

When to add the next level:

When your Quarterly Planning starts surfacing year-long issues. When you realize you're solving the same strategic problems every quarter because you're not planning far enough ahead.

Time to add Annual Planning.

Stage 4: Scale (Quarter-to-Quarter, Year-to-Year)

You're building a culture sustaining growth. Developing a Senior Leadership Team. Making sure your systems reinforce your purpose. You're thinking quarters to years.

What meetings you need:

All of the Stage 3 meetings, plus:

Board Meetings (if applicable): Quarterly or as needed.

State of the Company: Quarterly. Whole company. Leadership shares vision, progress, wins, and challenges. Keep everyone connected to where you're going. This is different from All-Hands. State of the Company is strategic. All-Hands is more operational.

All-Hands Meetings: Keep the company connected. Monthly or quarterly.

The trap: Adding meetings without killing old ones. Your calendar bloats. Audit ruthlessly. Every meeting earns the spot.

When to add the next level:

When you start thinking about legacy. When you're building something to outlast you. When you're asking, "What does this company look like in ten years?

Stage 5: Exit or Legacy (Year-to-Year, Decade-to-Decade)

You're thinking about legacy. Not as an endpoint, but as a living system. You're shaping a company outlasting you. Ten-year horizon and beyond.

What meetings you need:

All of Stage 4, plus:

Strategic Planning Sessions: Beyond Annual Planning. Multi-year vision work. Where is this company going long-term?

Board Meetings: Regular. Strategic. Governance-focused.

Succession Planning Conversations: Who's taking over? How do we build leaders who build leaders?

The focus shifts:
Less about doing the work. More about building the system. Your meetings reflect this. Less tactical. More strategic. More focused on culture, leadership development, and long-term thinking.

The trap: Losing touch with the front lines. You're thinking decades, but your company still lives week to week. Stay connected to all levels.

How to Know When to Add a Meeting

You don't add meetings because other companies have them. You add meetings when the pain of not having them becomes obvious. Here's the rule: If you're asking, "Should we have a meeting for this?" the answer is yes. But if you're asking, "Do we really need this meeting?" the answer is no.

How to Know When to Kill a Meeting

Meetings should die when they stop serving a purpose.
Here are the signals:

- Kill the meeting when: The same three people dominate every time, and everyone else checks out.

- Kill the meeting when: You finish in 15 minutes, but scheduled 60 because "this is what we do."

- Kill the meeting when: People schedule conflicts to avoid showing up.

- Kill the meeting when: You leave every week with no decisions, no actions, no clarity.

- Kill the meeting when: The meeting exists because someone put the thing on the calendar three years ago, and nobody questioned why.

Calendar Audit: Once a year, look at every recurring meeting on your calendar. Ask: Does this still serve us? If you hesitate, kill the thing.

Meeting Your Company Where It Is

The biggest mistake I see is leaders running meetings for the company they want to be, not the company they are. Stage 1 companies trying to run Level 10 Meetings. Stage 4 companies still operating like startups. Both fail. Your meetings need to match your stage. And as you grow, your meetings grow with you.

Start simple. Add structure when you need it. Kill meetings when they stop working. The goal isn't to have every meeting. The goal is to have the right meetings for where you are right now. Meet your company where the company is. Then grow together.

"Meetings Suck Less" Realization

Not every company needs every meeting. The meetings you need depend on your stage of development. Don't run meetings for the company you want to be. Run meetings for the company you are. Add structure when you feel the pain of not having the structure. Kill meetings when they stop serving you. Meet your company where the company is. Then grow together.

Next: You know the meeting format's working. But there's still one variable wrecking even the best agenda. And the variable might be you.

11

YES, YOU'RE THE PROBLEM (BUT THAT'S FIXABLE)

Here's a truth most leaders don't want to hear: if your meetings suck, there's a decent chance you're the reason. Not entirely. Not always. But more than you think.

I know this stings. Nobody wakes up thinking, "Today I'm going to run a terrible meeting and waste everyone's time." But intention doesn't matter when the result is the same. People leave confused. Issues don't get solved. The same problems keep showing up week after week. And if you're running the meeting? You own those problems.

The good news is you can fix this. But first, you have to look in the mirror and admit you might be the problem.

Assume You're Part of the Problem

LOOK IN THE MIRROR

ASK YOURSELF **HONESTLY**

- ☐ Do I interrupt people without realizing it?
- ☐ Do I give solutions before the team discusses?
- ☐ Do I redirect conversations to what I think matters?
- ☐ Do I dominate the airtime?
- ☐ Does my body language say "I'm bored"?
- ☐ Do I check my phone during meetings?
- ☐ Do the same issues keep coming back?
- ☐ Do people seem confused after meetings I run?

IF YOU CHECKED **3+**: You're probably part of the **problem**.
(But that's fixable.)

"Nobody wakes up thinking, **'Today I'll waste everyone's time.'**
But **intention** doesn't matter when the result is the same."

This is hard. We're all the heroes of our own stories. We see our intentions. We know how hard we're trying. We're aware of all the constraints we're dealing with. The budget cuts, the difficult team members, the impossible deadlines.

But your team doesn't see all this. They see results. Or lack of them.

So here's where you start: assume you're causing at least some of the issues. Not to beat yourself up. Not to spiral into imposter syndrome. But because this is true. And if you go into your self-assessment with this mindset, you'll find the stuff you need to fix.

I worked with a Visionary once who swore his meetings were fine. "My team doesn't speak up enough," he told me. "They're too passive."

I sat in on one of his Level 10 Meetings. Within fifteen minutes, I saw the problem. Every time someone brought up an issue, he'd interrupt with the solution. Every time someone started to discuss an idea, he'd redirect to what he thought mattered more. He was so focused on being efficient that he steamrolled every conversation.

After the meeting, I asked him, "Do you know how many times you interrupted people?"

He looked genuinely confused. "I didn't interrupt. I was moving things along."

This is the thing about being the problem. You don't see it from the inside.

The Politicking Problem

You know what kills meetings? Politicking. You've seen this. Someone says something insightful. Then another person jumps in with "Yeah, what Sarah said," and proceeds to take the next five minutes re-discussing everything Sarah said when she said it fine the first time.

I've been that person. I had nothing else to add, but I'm sucking the air out of the room. Going on this filibuster moment for no reason other than I think I should. And this is a distraction. People roll their eyes, thinking, "Damn, here we go again. No value add."

The worst part? This becomes contagious. If one person does this, others think, well, if they did this, then I should do this too. So they do. Then someone else goes, "Yeah, what Kris and Sarah said," and repeats everything again. And we didn't say anything new. There's no additional value in this moment.

The other problem is even worse. Someone says, "Yeah, what Sarah said," and then explains something completely different. Something competing with what Sarah said. But they're leveraging Sarah's intellectual capital and brand in the room.

I've seen this too. I'm sitting there thinking, "Wait a minute, she didn't say this at all. She said something completely different, and you're leveraging what she said as a jump-off point."

Call this out when you see this. Redirect. Move on.

When Command and Control Won't Let Go

Here's the big problem as companies scale: a leader or Visionary has success in Stage 1 and 2 with command and control. They tell everyone what to do. And then this stops working. They don't get to Stage 3 and beyond. They're trying to have everything.

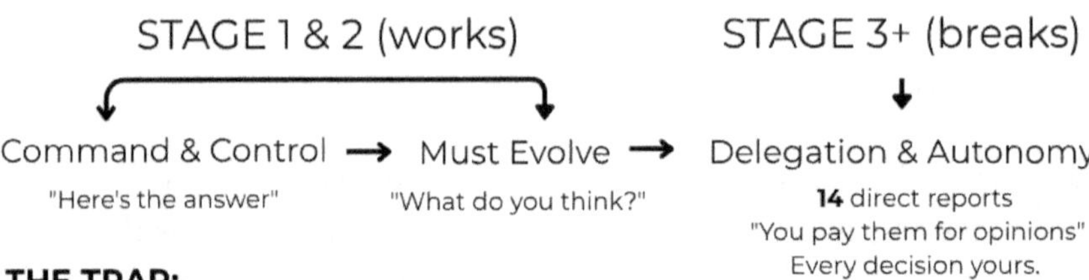

THE TRAP:
Success at Stage 1-2 with command & control
→ Leader tries to maintain it at Stage 3+
→ Team can't scale
→ Nothing gets done without you

THE SHIFT:
"You pay these people for their opinion. If you
don't want their opinion, **stop paying them**."

LETTING GO ≠ LOSING CONTROL
It's gaining capacity

I have a client right now with fourteen direct reports. He still dominates every conversation. When we get into IDS, I try to go around the room one at a time to open this up for discussion, and he will stop me. "This is a waste of time. Here's the answer."

I've pulled him aside multiple times. "Look, you pay these people. You've heard me say this. You pay them for an opinion. If you don't want their opinion, stop paying them. This doesn't make sense to me."

This change, from command and control to delegation and autonomy at the edges, is one of the hardest shifts a Visionary has to make.

The Ownership Problem

This is part of Lencioni's Five Dysfunctions of a Team. We talk about healthy conflict, then commit. But here's what leaders don't realize: disagreement shouldn't mean, "Okay, now I will just separate myself from what everyone else agreed to." Leaders should get them to commit to that solution even if they disagree.

Because you're like, "Well, okay, I'll do this. I'll go through the motions, but yeah, I think this is stupid."

If you want me to own this, you have to let me decide on it, to some degree. Say we are arguing about whether to call the book *Meetings Shouldn't Suck* or *Meetings Do Suck*, and at the end of the day, you tell me it has to be *Meetings Do Suck*. Now, if it doesn't perform, I can blame you, saying, "Yeah, you did this. I didn't decide this, even if it's my name on the cover."

This is the latitude to fail that leaders struggle with. We've done a better job at Ninety talking about one-way and two-way doors. If a decision is a two-way door, meaning things swing up and swing back, then please, let them decide so they own this. If a decision is a one-way door, and there's no coming back from this decision, well then, yeah, this should be at the right escalation point and decision rights. And the person has to own this if things go wrong.

Watch Yourself (No, For Real)

If you have the ability to record your meetings, do this. Then watch yourself. I know. This is painful. Nobody likes seeing themselves on video. You'll hate the sound of your voice. You'll notice every weird tic. You'll cringe. Do this anyway.

Because you'll also notice things you didn't know you were doing. You're checking your phone more than you realize. You're cutting people off. Your body language is screaming "I'm bored" even though you think you're engaged.

One of my clients recorded a quarterly planning session. When he watched this back, he was horrified. "I looked checked out for half the meeting. No wonder people don't bring their best ideas. I'm signaling to them I don't care." He didn't realize he was doing this in the moment. But the video didn't lie.

If recording isn't an option, ask someone you trust to observe and give you feedback. A peer. A coach. Someone who will tell you the truth. You need an objective view. Because your internal narrative is wrong.

When Leaders Shut Down Meetings Without Realizing Things

When leaders have a dominating trait, they start to dominate the situation when they get triggered. And people pull back. They're like, "Okay, well, if you feel this strongly…"

I don't know if the dominating leaders always see themselves doing this. They're emotive and passionate. They've seen this before. They don't want to risk whatever happened last time happening again. So they think they're doing the right thing.

People have triggers. Did people get yelled at at home? I don't know. Was silence a weapon? I don't know. All these things happen.

I had one situation where the leader would sit in silence. Complete silence. I'd be sitting there thinking, "What are we doing? Why is he not saying anything? The rest of the team is sitting there, waiting for him to speak. Is he going to say anything? What the hell?"

But this was his weapon. He would use this and make everyone uncomfortable in silence, rather than yelling. This was hard. Because they were trained to wait until he said something. And this was not productive at all.

This didn't last. I think we did a couple quarters, and then it was over. The system was not working for them because they weren't working it. The system does work, but if you choose not to apply it, then you don't get to complain when this doesn't work.

The Quarterly Self-Audit

Here's a practice for you: once a quarter, review your meeting performance. Block time on your calendar. Call this "Meeting Performance Review" or whatever, won't make you want to skip this.

Pull up your meeting ratings from the past 90 days. If you're running Level 10 Meetings, you're already rating them 1 to 10 at the end of every session. Look at the pattern. Are ratings trending up or down? Are they consistently low? Are there specific weeks where things tanked?

Then ask yourself:

- What was different in the high-rated meetings versus the low-rated ones?

- What issues kept coming back that we didn't solve?

- Did I cut anyone off?

- Did I let someone dominate?

- Did I rush through IDS because I had "more important" things to do?

Write down your answers. Then turn them into to-dos. Specific, measurable improvements you're going to make next quarter.

For example: "I talked too much in IDS. Next quarter, I'm going to wait five seconds after someone finishes talking before I respond."

Or: "I let the same three people dominate every meeting. Next quarter, I'm going to ask the quiet people for their input."

This isn't about perfection. This is about getting 1 percent better every quarter. The improvement will compound.

I've been doing this for years. Every quarter, I review my facilitation. Every quarter, I find something to improve. Some quarters, this is small. "I need to be better at time boxing." Other quarters, this is big. "I need to let the team solve problems without me jumping in."

The practice keeps me honest. And this keeps my meetings from sliding back into mediocrity.

When you stop just thinking about improvement and start writing something down, you're creating accountability for yourself. You're not hoping to get better. You're tracking this. You're measuring this. And you're building improvement into your own Rocks.

One client started doing this and discovered a pattern. His meetings were always better in weeks where he'd reviewed the Issues List the night before. Obvious in hindsight, but he'd never connected the dots. Now he blocks thirty minutes every Monday evening for prep. His meeting ratings jumped from 6s to 8s in a single quarter.

Small changes. Consistent practice. This is how you get better.

QUARTERLY MEETING AUDIT
DO THIS EVERY 90 DAYS

(1) What's the purpose?

Can't articulate it?	➜	KILL IT
Clear purpose?	➜	CONTINUE

(2) Is it being achieved?

NO	➜	FIX IT or KILL IT
YES	➜	CONTINUE

(3) Can you draw line to the ROI?

NO	➜	KILL IT
YES	➜	KEEP IT

(4) What breaks if we cancel?

Nothing?	➜	KILL IT
Something specific?	➜	REDESIGN around that

(✗) Kate's 1-on-1: Started with great intentions (she was new), but now? Other meetings cover it. → **KILLED**

(✓) Mentorship 1-on-1s: Developing people outside your direct area → **KEEP** (but audit periodically)

The Emotion Problem

Here's what often happens: people want to spend more than five minutes on the Scorecard. If it's an issue, it needs to be dropped down to IDS. But because there is emotion attached to the issue, they want to talk about it right now.

What they don't want to do is break the pattern of the emotion. Because if they're emotive in the moment, they want to talk about this. I assure them we will talk about it, I promise. This is going to be there. We'll prioritize this. We will get to this. But right now, we're not going to do this. This kind of pattern-break is hard.

You Shouldn't Facilitate

Here's a question requiring courage: Should you even be facilitating this meeting? Being the boss doesn't mean you're the best person to run every meeting. In fact, there are times when your presence as facilitator hurts the dynamic.

I worked with a Visionary once who loved running the weekly leadership team meeting. But he was terrible at it. He'd go off on tangents. He'd get excited about new ideas and derail the agenda. The team would leave more confused than when they started.

His Integrator finally said, "I think I should run the L10. You bring great energy, but we need more structure."

The Visionary's first reaction was defensiveness. "Are you saying I don't know how to run a meeting?"

The Integrator was smart. She didn't make this about capability. She made this about fit. "You're great at casting vision and challenging us. But when you're also trying to keep us on track, you do neither of these well. Let me handle the structure so you can focus on the ideas."

He agreed to try this for 90 days. And guess what? The meetings got better. Way better. The Visionary still participated. Still brought his energy and ideas. But now someone else was keeping the train on the tracks.

If you're struggling to facilitate, hand this off. This isn't a failure. This is self-awareness. And sometimes, the best thing you do for your team is get out of your own way.

The Facilitator's Job (Are You Doing This?)

Let's review what a facilitator is supposed to do:

- Keep the meeting on track
- Make sure everyone gets heard
- Drive to decisions
- Manage time
- Create space for healthy conflict

You're not there to have all the answers. You're not there to be the smartest person in the room. You're there to make sure the meeting accomplishes what this is supposed to accomplish. So ask yourself: are you doing this?

Or are you doing this:

- Jumping in with solutions before the team has a chance to discuss
- Letting the loudest voice win
- Avoiding conflict because it is uncomfortable
- Letting conversations meander because you don't want to seem controlling
- Talking more than everyone else combined

Be honest. Because if you're doing the second list, you're not facilitating. You're in charge of a meeting, and it's not going to work.

Here's a helpful exercise: after your next meeting, estimate how much you talked versus how much everyone else talked. If you talked more than 30 percent of the time, you talked too much.

Your job is to create the conditions for good conversation. Not to dominate it.

Are You Getting to the Root Cause?

One of the most common facilitation failures is surface-level IDS. Someone brings an issue. You discuss this for five minutes. Someone suggests a solution. You assign a to-do. You move on. Except you didn't solve anything. You solved a symptom.

Let me give you an example. A team brings up the issue: "We're missing deadlines."

Surface-level IDS: "Okay, let's all commit to better time management. Sarah, send a reminder email when deadlines are coming up."

Root cause IDS: "Why are we missing deadlines? Is this capacity? Is this unclear priorities? Is this scope creep? Is this a skills gap? Let's dig into this."

The first approach feels efficient. You solved this in five minutes. But the issue will be back next week because you didn't solve the problem.

The second approach takes longer. Twenty minutes. But when you're done, you've identified the root cause. Let's say this is scope creep. And you solve this permanently by getting better at defining project scope upfront.

As a facilitator, your job is to ask the follow-up questions. To push past the easy answer. To make the team uncomfortable for a few minutes so you solve the issue for real.

If the same issues keep showing up in your meetings, you're not getting to the root cause. And that is on you.

Handling Interruptions and Derailments

Every meeting has interruptions. Someone's phone rings. Someone brings up a tangent. Someone starts telling a five-minute story having nothing to do with the issue at hand. How you handle these moments defines whether your meeting works or not.

Here's what doesn't work:

- Letting tangents take over because you don't want to seem rude
- Snapping at people when they go off-topic
- Ignoring interruptions and hoping they stop

Here's what does work:

- Acknowledge the tangent: "Interesting, but this isn't the issue we're solving right now. Add this to the Issues List."
- Redirect gently but firmly: "Let's stay focused on the issue at hand. We'll come back to this if there's time."
- Use the Issues List: "Great point. Let's capture this as a separate issue and tackle this later."

I once coached a team where the facilitator let every conversation spiral. Someone would mention a customer complaint, and suddenly they're redesigning the entire product roadmap. Fifteen minutes later, nobody remembers what issue they were even supposed to be solving.

I taught him a simple trick: when someone goes off-topic, say, "This is an issue. Let's add this to the list." Then physically write this down. This signals to the person their idea matters, but this also gets the meeting back on track.

Within a month, his meetings were 30 percent shorter and way more effective.

Know When You're at Your Best (And When You're Not)

Not every meeting is created equal. And you're not equally good at facilitating all of them.

Maybe you're great at running Level 10 Meetings but terrible at facilitating brainstorms. You're sharp in the morning but lose focus after lunch. You're better when you've prepped and worse when you're winging this. Pay attention to these patterns.

I know I'm at my best when I've reviewed the Issues List before the meeting. When I know what we're walking into. When I've had coffee. When I'm not stressed about ten other things. I'm at my worst when I'm rushed. When I didn't prep. When I'm trying to facilitate while also solving a crisis.

Once you know your patterns, design around them. Schedule your most important meetings when you're sharp. Prep more for the meetings where you tend to struggle. And if you know you're off your game, be honest with the team: "I'm not at my best today, so I need you all to help keep us on track."

Once you know your patterns, design around them.

This kind of vulnerability builds trust. Because your team already knows when you're off. Naming this makes this easier for everyone to adjust.

Who's in the Room (And Are You Drawing Them Out?)

Look around your next meeting. Who's talking? Who's not? If the same three people dominate every conversation, you're not facilitating well. If the quietest person hasn't spoken in three weeks, you're not facilitating well.

Your job is to create space for everyone. Not the loud ones. Not the confident ones. Everyone. Here are some tactics:

Direct questions: "Jen, you've been quiet. What's your take on this?"

Round-robins: "Let's go around the table. Everyone gets 60 seconds to weigh in."

Pre-work: Send the Issues List before the meeting so introverts have time to think.

One of my clients had a sales leader who never spoke up in the leadership team meeting. Turns out, this wasn't because he didn't have ideas. This was because the pace of conversation was so fast he couldn't get a word in.

I asked the facilitator to slow down. To pause after each person spoke. To invite the sales leader into the conversation.

Within two meetings, he was contributing regularly. And his ideas were good. But for months, the team had missed out because the facilitator wasn't creating space.

Gather Feedback (And Listen to It)

Here's the scary part: Ask your team how you're doing. Not in a passive, "Hey, how are meetings going?" kind of way. In a direct, "I want honest feedback on my facilitation" kind of way.

You do this in your Quarterly Conversations. You do this in a team retrospective. You do this anonymously if this feels safer.

Ask questions like:

- What's one thing I do well in meetings?
- What's one thing I can improve?
- Do you feel like you get a chance to contribute?
- Do you feel like your ideas are heard?
- Is there anything I do that shuts down conversation?

Then, and this is the hard part, listen. Don't defend. Don't explain. Don't justify. Listen.

One Visionary I worked with did this and got some tough feedback. "You cut people off. A lot. And when you do, they stop trying to contribute."

His first instinct was to say, "But I'm trying to move things along!" Instead, he said, "Thank you. I didn't realize I was doing this. I'm going to work on this."

Next meeting, he caught himself mid-interruption. He stopped. He said, "Sorry, I did the thing. Finish your thought." The team laughed. He got better. And the meetings improved.

Feedback only works if you're willing to listen and change.

For Leaders: Build Your Meeting EQ

Emotional intelligence isn't only for one-on-ones. This matters in group meetings, too.

You need to be able to read the room. To notice when someone's checked out. To see when someone's frustrated but not saying this. To catch the tension before this turns into dysfunction.

Here's what to watch for:

- Body language: Who's leaning in? Who's leaning back? Who's looking at their phone?
- Energy levels: Who's engaged? Who's exhausted? Who's about to snap?
- Participation patterns: Who's talking? Who's silent? Who's dominating?
- Conflict avoidance: Is someone biting their tongue? Are people agreeing too quickly?

I've been in meetings where you feel the tension. Someone's pissed. Everyone knows this. But nobody's saying anything. And the facilitator plows ahead like everything's fine. This is low meeting EQ.

High meeting EQ looks like this: "I can tell something's off. What's going on?"

This is uncomfortable. But this is better than ignoring the elephant in the room and having this blow up later.

One of my favorite facilitation moves is the mid-meeting check-in. If I sense the energy's off, I'll pause and say, "How's everyone doing? Are we solving the right stuff, or are we spinning?"

Nine times out of ten, someone will say what everyone's thinking. And then we address this.

For Participants: Your Role in This

Okay, enough about facilitators. Let's talk about the other participants.

If you're sitting in meetings, you have responsibility too. You don't get to show up, zone out, and blame the facilitator when nothing happens.

Here are some hard questions to ask yourself:

Would people care if I wasn't here?

Seriously. If you disappeared from this meeting, would anyone notice? Would the meeting be worse? Or would it be better because there's one less person taking up space?

If you don't have a confident answer to this question, you either need to add more value or stop attending.

The truth is, you may no longer need to be in the meeting, or never did to begin with. Someone added you to the invite three years ago, and you've been showing up ever since, even though you don't contribute and don't get value.

If this is true, ask to opt out. Talk to the facilitator. Say, "I don't think I need to be in this meeting anymore. Remove me from the invite."

Most of the time, they'll say yes. Because they don't want you there if you don't need to be there either.

Why don't I speak up?

If you're consistently silent, why? Are you afraid of what people will think? Do you not understand what's being discussed? Are you doing other work on the side? None of these are good reasons.

If you're afraid of judgment, this is a culture problem. Talk to your manager. If you don't understand, ask questions. This isn't weakness. This is engagement. If you're doing other work, stop. Either be present or don't be there.

Do I feel safe bringing up issues?

This is a big one. Permission to disagree is everything.

If you don't feel comfortable raising questions, disagreeing, or bringing conflict to the table, your meetings will never be productive because all the issues will stay hidden.

So ask yourself: Why don't I feel safe? Is this the culture? Is this a specific person? Is this something about how I've been treated in the past?

And then ask: What would make me feel safer? More structure? More clarity on expectations? A different facilitator?

You won't fix the culture alone. But you can name the problem. And this is the first step.

Do people not speak up because of me?

Here's a tough one: are you the reason other people stay quiet? You dominate every conversation. You shoot down ideas too quickly. You're dismissive when someone says something you think is obvious.

If people shut down when you're in the room, this is on you. Pay attention. Notice who stops talking when you start. Notice whose ideas get ignored after you've weighed in. And then back off. Let other people lead. Let other people's ideas breathe. Stop being the person everyone has to work around.

It's Not About Perfection

Let's be clear: you're not going to be perfect. Nobody is. You're going to have off days. You're going to interrupt people. You're going to miss cues. You're going to let a conversation spiral.

Fine. The goal isn't perfection. The goal is awareness and improvement. If you're paying attention, catching yourself, and getting better over time, you're doing this right.

But if you're ignoring the feedback, defending your bad habits, and blaming everyone else for why meetings suck, then yeah. You're the problem. The good news is, you can stop being the problem starting today.

The goal isn't perfection. The goal is awareness and improvement.

Look, I know these topics are uncomfortable. Nobody likes being told they're the issue. But if you made it this far, you care. You're willing to look in the mirror and do the hard work.

And this is exactly what separates good leaders from mediocre ones. Good leaders ask for feedback. They watch themselves. They adjust. They create space for others. They get better.

Mediocre leaders blame the team. They make excuses. They double down on what's not working. And they wonder why nothing ever changes. You don't have to be perfect. You have to be willing to do better.

"Meetings Suck Less" Realization

The meeting you're in says as much about the participant as the facilitator. If meetings suck and you're not speaking up, not bringing issues to the table, or not adding value, you're part of the problem. And if you're running the meeting and people leave confused, frustrated, or disengaged, own this reality. Start with assuming you're part of the issue. Get feedback. Adjust. Try again. This is how you stop being the problem and start being part of the solution.

Next: You've learned the formats. You've looked in the mirror. Now let's bring this all together and talk about why meetings don't have to suck and why yours won't anymore.

12

MEETINGS DON'T SUCK. YOURS DO.

Let's get one thing straight: Meetings don't suck. I'll argue this with anyone. Anywhere. Because I know the truth.

The concept of a meeting is brilliant. You get the right people in a room to solve problems, make decisions, and move the business forward. When you do this well, meetings become one of the most useful tools you have as a leader. They get fun. They get engaging. You feel rewarded by them.

But your meetings? Yeah, those suck. But you have the strength to fix them. I've spent this entire book being honest about what's broken. About the time you're wasting. About the frustration your team feels. About the ways you might be part of the problem. And if you've made it this far, you know I'm not here to blow sunshine. I'm here to tell you the truth.

So here goes: You don't have a meeting problem. You have an execution problem. The frameworks exist. The tools work. The formats are proven. Thousands of companies run great meetings right now. They use EOS. They follow the Level 10 Meeting structure. They solve issues with IDS. They set Rocks and track Scorecards and hold each other accountable.

I've seen this work hundreds of times. The question isn't whether you have the ability to fix your meetings. The question is whether you're willing to do the work.

Meetings Are Where Everything Happens

Here's what most people get wrong: They think meetings are separate from the "real work." Wrong.

Meetings are where strategy becomes execution. Meetings are where culture gets built or destroyed. Meetings are where you find out if your team has alignment or is pretending to have alignment.

Maybe you have the best vision in the world. You hire amazing people. You have a killer product and a solid business model. But if your meetings suck, none of this matters. Because meetings are where you turn ideas into action.

Think about this:

- Strategy gets decided in meetings.
- Problems get solved in meetings.
- Priorities get set in meetings.
- Accountability gets established in meetings.
- Culture gets reinforced or eroded in meetings.

Every week, your team gathers. And in those moments, you're either building momentum or bleeding out. You're either creating clarity or adding confusion. You're either solving issues or letting them fester.

There's no middle ground. Your meetings are either making your business better or making your business worse.

And here's what I know from working with 50-plus clients in over 400 session days: Meetings are a function of moving growth forward. We're trying to find the thing stopping our progress. We're trying to find the ceiling, the barrier, or whatever you want to call the obstacle. What needs to be true for us to move forward?

The Cost of Bad Meetings (Let's Do the Math One More Time)

I know we talked about this in Chapter 1. But I'm going to repeat this. If you have ten people in a meeting for an hour, each with an average salary of $100K, you're looking at roughly $500 in labor cost. Per meeting.

Now multiply this by every meeting your company runs in a week. Then a month. Then a year. Add in the opportunity cost. The work your people didn't get done. The decisions your team delayed. The issues your company didn't solve.

And then, this is the part where the pain gets real, add in the cultural cost. The frustration. The disengagement. The eye rolls. The "why am I even here" moments chipping away at trust and morale.

Bad meetings are expensive, way more expensive than most leaders realize. And all of this cost is optional. You're choosing to waste time, money, and morale by running meetings without structure. You have the option to choose differently tomorrow.

"But Kris, Is This Worth the Effort? We're Doing Okay."

Look, there are plenty of companies running lifestyle businesses, and I mean this respectfully. They make money, they grow at 3 percent a year, they stay above inflation, they pass out 1-3 percent raises to everybody on an annual basis, and they do what they do. If you want this and this is your desire, then Godspeed.

But so many leaders and entrepreneurs sign up for growth. They sign up for growth because "A-players" live there. The people who want to grow want to grow financially, professionally, personally. And "A-players" won't tolerate those lifestyle businesses. If they join them by mistake, they'll figure it out, and they'll be like, "I shouldn't be here anymore. I gotta go somewhere else for growth."

One of the core values for Professional EOS Implementers and EOS Worldwide is "grow or die". You will have entropy over time. The business will start to decline. People will leave. Not this year, but next year, or the year after, the decline happens. Most small businesses die because they didn't grow.

So I think the question becomes: You think you're doing okay? But is doing okay where growth lives?

The Thermometer vs. The Thermostat

Let me tell you something I've learned from facilitating more sessions than I count: You have two choices when you walk into a meeting. You become the thermometer, which means you tell the room what temperature you're feeling. Or you become the thermostat, and you set the temperature.

If I feel the energy's not right in a quarterly meeting, I'm gonna take a step back and say, "Hey team, this isn't right. I don't know, let's try to understand what's happening right now, but either you're tired, hungover, whatever the situation is. We have to acknowledge this is your most important day of the quarter."

I started doing this last year because I was intrigued by the idea. When everyone else checks in at a quarterly, I get to set expectations as a facilitator. And I say, "Well, I want you to be open, honest, vulnerable, create a plan you believe in, but I'm going to offer you an opportunity."

Then I pause. "Are you guys open to an opportunity?" They never say no.

"Does this have the potential to be the best quarterly we've ever had?"

They're like, "Oh yeah, sounds good."

"No, I mean it. Does this have the potential?"

"Okay, yes, yeah."

"Still not there. I'm gonna go around the room. I want to know if you're all in on making this the best quarterly we've ever done."

And this changes everything. Because I go, "Alright, Bob, are you all in?" Bob's like, "Yeah, man, I'm all in." "Good. Jessica, are you all in?"

Doing this last bit gets them committed. I've changed the energy. I don't always do this unless the energy's not right. Something's off here. They didn't get their workout in, they haven't had their coffee, I don't know. But the reason doesn't matter. I have to figure out how to change the situation.

The Three Things I've Seen Make the Biggest Difference

I've run a lot of meetings in my career. And if I'm honest, there are three moments making the biggest difference. Get these three things right, and the rest starts to fall into place.

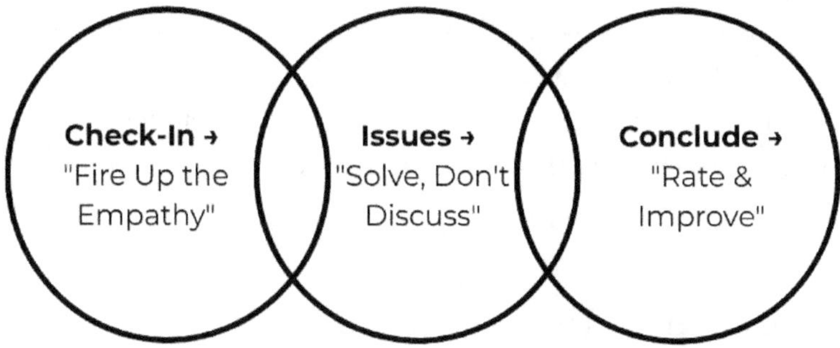

Non-Negotiable One: The Check-In At the Start

The check-in sets the tone. I always say these are empathy triggers. I'm trying to get you to fire the team up because we're going to get to the hard work of issue-solving, and I need everyone to know they are here doing the right work. You care about each other, you're connected.

Now, I don't let my clients get away with shallow check-ins. Everyone shares a personal and professional best. Let's go. And if I'm doing this as a facilitator, I say, "Personal, professional best, and tell me why. Of all the time you had this last quarter, why did you choose this one thing?"

This is the point.

If you say, "Well, I went to my kid's baseball game, and the game was good," I'm like, "Oh, awesome. Tell me why. Why, of all the things you have the option to choose, is this the one you're choosing to share right now?"

And I'm pushing to get to the last emotive part. And you're like, "This is important for me because my mom never went to any of my baseball games."

Boom. Now I've got the answer. This is why the moment is important to you, and this is why you shared the story. Now, this connection changes everything in the room.

Non-Negotiable Two: Issues

If we don't figure out the things keeping us from progressing, and we don't have an action item, a line of sight to the next thing we need to do to move forward, then we don't make progress. So Issues is the second non-negotiable for every meeting.

This is where IDS happens. This is where the real work gets done. And you have to protect this time. You have to make sure you're solving things, not discussing things.

Non-Negotiable Three: Conclude

If we didn't do the meeting well, or we didn't do the meeting right, and we don't want to make the next one better, then we have problems. But if I get to conclude, and people are rating the meeting 9, but you rate it a 6?

Let's talk about your 6. Because your 6 is real, and the score is your truth, not mine. I'm not judging your 6. I want to understand the rating, so if there's something we can do better and different, we're going to deal with the issue.

Everything discussed beyond these three elements is important too, don't get me wrong, but we've gotta get these three nailed for sure in order to make something happen.

What Good Meetings Look Like

Let me paint you a picture.

Monday morning arrives. Your leadership team walks into the conference room, or your team logs into the Zoom call, for your weekly Level

10 Meeting. Everyone's on time. Everyone's prepared. Everyone knows the agenda.

You start with segue. Five minutes of good news. Personal and professional. This gets everyone present, connected, and in the right headspace.

Someone shares their kid made the soccer team. Someone else talks about landing a new client. Another person mentions they fixed the thing driving them crazy for weeks. Simple. Human. And this shifts the energy from "another meeting" to "we're in this together."

Then you review the Scorecard. Five minutes. No storytelling. Data only. Are we on or off track? If we're off, we add the issue to the Issues List and move on.

Rock review. Two minutes per Rock. On track or off track. If anything is off track, why? What needs to happen? Add the issue to the Issues List and move on.

Customer and employee headlines. Anything the team needs to know. Quick updates. No deep dives. If the topic needs discussion, add the topic to the Issues List.

Then the To-Do List. Did you do what you said you'd do last week? Yes or no. No excuses. No explanations. Accountability only.

And now, the main event. The Issues List. This is where 60 percent of your meeting time should go. This is where you solve real problems. This is where you use IDS to identify the root cause, discuss the cause, and solve the problem.

You tackle the most important issues first. You stay disciplined. You don't go down rabbit holes. And when you solve something, you create a To-Do and move on.

You conclude. Everyone rates the meeting on a scale of 1-10. You take feedback. You commit to making next week's meeting even better.

Total time? 90 minutes. And you got more done than you did in five hours of other meetings last week.

This is what's available to you. This is what a great meeting looks like. And this is not theory. This is practice. Hundreds of companies are doing this every single week.

What's on the Line

You know what happens when you fix your meetings? Everything changes. You get your time back. Your team gets aligned. Problems get solved. Momentum builds. And suddenly, the business you're trying to build becomes the business you have.

Meetings are a forever work.

This is what's on the line. A better business. A better culture. A better experience for everyone who shows up to work every day. You deserve this. Your team deserves this. And the outcome sits within reach.

Here's what I want you to acknowledge: Meetings are a forever work.

You don't want to learn a skill and let the skill go. Anytime you learn something new, if you choose to play the game, then this is a skill you have to keep mastering.

You have to reflect upon the skill. You have to make sure you're prepared for the work. Come with energy. Treat the process respectfully. Because meetings are not something to get through. Meetings are something to do.

And if you prepare right and you execute well, then you're gonna feel all the uplift around the work.

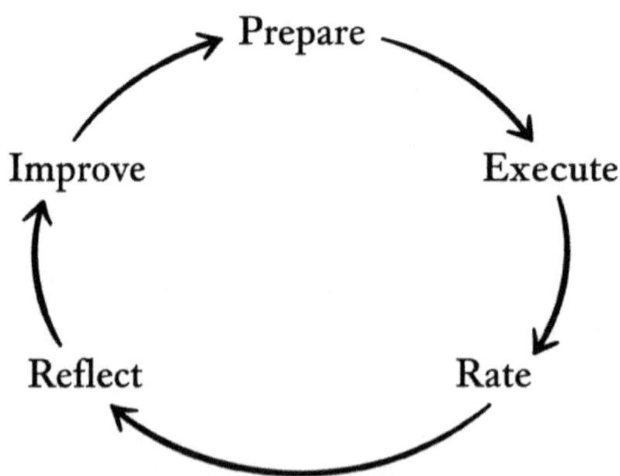

**Meetings don't get fixed once.
They get better every week.**

I want you to walk away from this book thinking, "The possibilities are endless. We're gonna improve so much in how we do all these different types of meetings, and they won't suck anymore, because we're gonna do the work differently."

Some meetings suck. But if we do something different, then they don't have to suck. You have the optimism. We do this differently tomorrow. I want to leave you with one last story. A few years ago, I worked with a Visionary who was about to quit. Not retire. Quit. Walk away from the company he'd spent fifteen years building.

Why? Because the work wasn't fun anymore. The business had become a grind. Meetings were exhausting. Nothing ever seemed to get resolved. He was working 70-hour weeks and still felt like he was falling behind.

I asked him to give me 90 days—three months—to fix the meetings. If the approach didn't work, he walks away guilt-free.

He agreed. We implemented Level 10 Meetings. Weekly pulse. Disciplined format. IDS for issue solving. At first, he was skeptical. "This feels too structured. Too rigid." I told him to trust the process.

By week 12, he was a different person. Energized. Engaged. Enjoying the work again. You know what he told me?

"I forgot what this felt like to love running this company. The meetings gave me my business back."

This is what's available to you. Getting your business back. Getting your time back. Getting your joy back. And this starts with one meeting. This week.

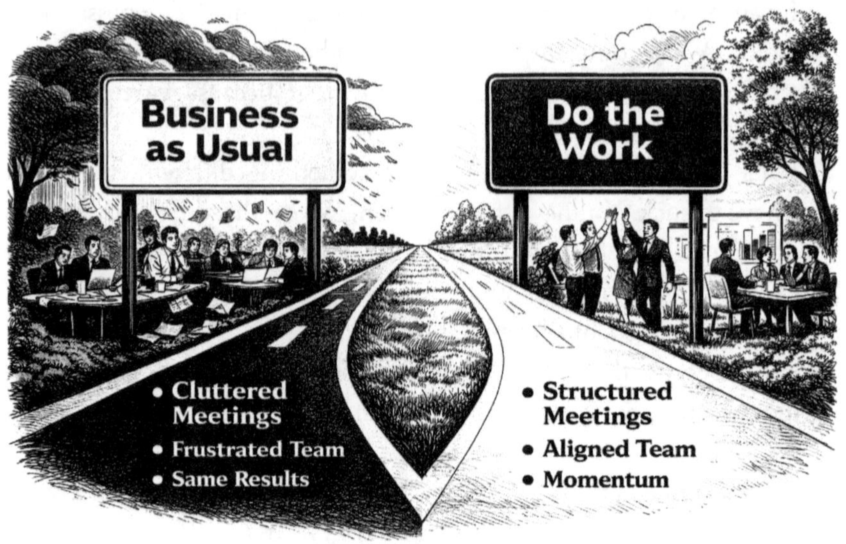

Your Two Paths Forward

What Happens Next

Next, you close this book. And then you have a choice. You can go back to business as usual. Keep running the same meetings. Keep getting the same results. Keep wondering why things aren't changing. Or you can decide today is the day things change.

Your meetings suck. And you own this. But you have the ability to fix them. You know the format. You know the tools. You know what works. The only question is whether you are willing to do the work.

Block time this week to prep for your next Level 10 Meeting. Send the agenda to your team. Show up ready. Run the meeting well. Rate the meeting at the end. Then do this again next week.

And in 90 days, look back. I promise you'll see the difference. Your meetings will be sharper. Your team will be clearer. Your business will be moving faster.

The business and the life you want sit on the other side of meetings that work well. So go run a great meeting. Then run another one. And another one. And watch what happens.

"Meetings Suck Less" Realization

Meetings don't suck. Yours do. And this is great news. Because you have the strength to fix them. You don't need a bigger budget, a different team, or a complete overhaul of your business. You need to commit to doing meetings differently. Pick a format. Show up prepared. Solve real issues. Hold people accountable. Do this consistently for 90 days and watch what happens. Your meetings will stop sucking. Your team will get aligned. Your business will move faster. And you'll get your time and your sanity back. This is a forever work. Meetings are a skill you have to keep mastering. But if you're willing to do the work, the possibilities are endless. Not hope. A promise.

A FINAL NOTE

Thanks for reading. Seriously. You could have spent this time in another pointless meeting. But instead, you invested it in learning how to fix them.

Now go prove it wasn't a waste of time. Run a Level 10 Meeting this week. Rate it. Adjust. Do it again.

And if you need help, reach out. I'm at kris@ninety.io or Kris.Snyder@eosworldwide.com. I love hearing from people who are doing the work.

Here's to meetings that don't suck.

ACKNOWLEDGMENTS

Books don't get written alone. Even when you're the one staring at a blank screen at 6 a.m., questioning all your choices.

First, to the leadership teams I've had the privilege of coaching. You're in these pages. Not by name, but your stories, your breakthroughs, your stubbornness, your courage — all of it's here. You trusted me in the room. You did the hard work. You let me push back when things got uncomfortable. This book exists because of what you taught me. Thank you.

To the EOS community — the Implementers, Visionaries, Integrators, and coaches doing this work every single day. You are proof that a great operating system, in the hands of committed people, changes companies. And lives. I'm proud to be part of this.

To the team at Ninety — thank you for building a tool that supports this work at scale. What you're doing matters more than most people realize. Meetings get better when the infrastructure behind them is built right, and you've built something that helps teams do that well.

To Audra Stanton, who contributed Chapter 6 of this book and helped bring my stories to life. You brought science to a subject most people treat as opinion. You made it smarter. Thank you for saying yes and making this book great.

To Mark Abbott, Founder and Visionary of Ninety. I met Mark when he had a small team and a conviction that there should be software to bring operating systems to life. He was right. Mark is a product-led founder who obsesses over what users need. His work on trust has affected how I coach teams, and his belief that companies should be productive, humane, and resilient isn't a tagline. He lives the thing. Thank you for building something worth fighting for.

To the people at Impact Architects who have been in the trenches with me — building, coaching, learning, and occasionally surviving the meetings that didn't work. You know who you are.

To my family — who sat through 22 years of dinner conversations about leadership, teams, and why that Monday meeting is still broken. You never stopped asking questions. That's a gift I don't take lightly.

And finally, to you — whoever picked up this book. Whether meetings are currently sucking the life out of your organization or you're just looking to make good ones great, I'm glad you're here. Let's fix this together.

ABOUT THE AUTHOR

Kris Snyder is a seasoned entrepreneur, Professional EOS Implementer®, and growth strategist who serves as the Chief Revenue Officer (CRO) at Ninety.io, where he leads revenue growth, partner development, and customer success initiatives for one of the fastest-growing SaaS companies. With over 25 years of executive experience, Kris has built, led, scaled, and sold multiple companies—and now  helps others do the same with clarity, discipline, and heart.

As CRO, Kris has played a pivotal role in expanding Ninety's reach and accelerating its mission to help organizations become more productive, humane, and resilient. He has spearheaded the development of Ninety's partner ecosystem, cultivating deep relationships with EOS Implementers, business coaches, and entrepreneurial advisors across the globe. Under his leadership, Ninety's partner network of over 2,000 coaches and advisors has grown significantly in size, impact, and integration—establishing the company as a vital tool for advisors who help leadership teams gain traction and scale.

Kris also leads Ninety's Client Experience and Revenue teams, aligning product value with customer outcomes and championing a people-first approach to client success for the over 16,000 clients. His leadership ensures that every touchpoint—from onboarding to ongoing enablement—reinforces Ninety's promise to deliver clarity, simplicity, and trust.

Prior to joining Ninety, Kris founded and led Vox Mobile, a technology services company that scaled to over 200 employees, raised more than $30 million in growth capital, and became an industry leader in managed mobility. His entrepreneurial background also includes founding or advising multiple ventures in SaaS, business services, and professional coaching. He understands the growth journey from the inside—and brings that empathy to every leader he works with.

As the Founder and Managing Partner of Impact Architects, Kris has facilitated over 400 EOS® session days for leadership teams seeking to break through growth ceilings. He's a trusted mentor to business owners navigating complexity, scale, and succession.

Kris is a frequent speaker at national leadership conferences—including the EOS Conference—and a regular contributor to Ninety's thought leadership on strategy, culture, team health, and scaling systems. His writing and speaking emphasize the power of building great companies by aligning people, process, and purpose—and by leaning into trust as a core business competency.

Calm, candid, and values-driven, Kris brings a rare combination of entrepreneurial grit, systems expertise, and relational intelligence to every room he's in. Whether advising founders, building partnerships, or scaling revenue teams, he is consistently focused on helping others build enduring organizations that are not only successful but deeply worth working for.

GUEST CONTRIBUTOR

Audra Stanton, M.D., is Head of Product at Ninety with a unique background in medicine and academics, having transitioned from clinical practice to leadership roles in product and technology stemming from a strong desire to make a more impactful difference in our world. Previously, she was an EdTech leader, serving as Chief Academic and Innovation Officer at Revolution Prep, ensuring products were grounded in research-based pedagogy and featured innovative learning

approaches. An executive, educator, and strategist with expertise spanning SaaS, healthcare, neuroscience, and AI, she is a true innovator with a passion for building effective teams and scaling organizations. Her focus is on transforming what we know to be "learning" and "work" so that humans can achieve more than they imagined.

Dr. Stanton earned both her Bachelor of Science and her Doctor of Medicine degrees from The George Washington University. She trained as a physician specializing in psychiatry at the Cleveland Clinic Akron General and Summa Health System, with research published in leading journals including the *Journal of Neuroscience*, the *European Journal of Emergency Medicine*, the *Journal of Ultrasound in Medicine*, and *Academic Emergency Medicine*. She is also a graduate of Seth Godin's altMBA program.

Forbes has featured her insights on the future of work, side hustles, workplace trends, and how AI is transforming how we work. *Training Magazine* has highlighted her perspectives on continuous learning, vulnerable leadership, and change management. *Emotional Intelligence Magazine* has featured her expertise on test anxiety and performance under pressure.

Beyond her work as an executive, she teaches undergraduate science courses at Robert Morris University in her spare time. A lover of both art and science, she finds joy outside of work in modern dance, reading, playing the piano, and creative invention. She lives in the Pittsburgh, PA area with her husband, Owen, and their son, Lachlan.

GROW INTENTIONALLY.
EXIT SUBSTANTIALLY.

Proven processes, expertise & technology that enable growth-oriented entrepreneurs to grow and exit by design.

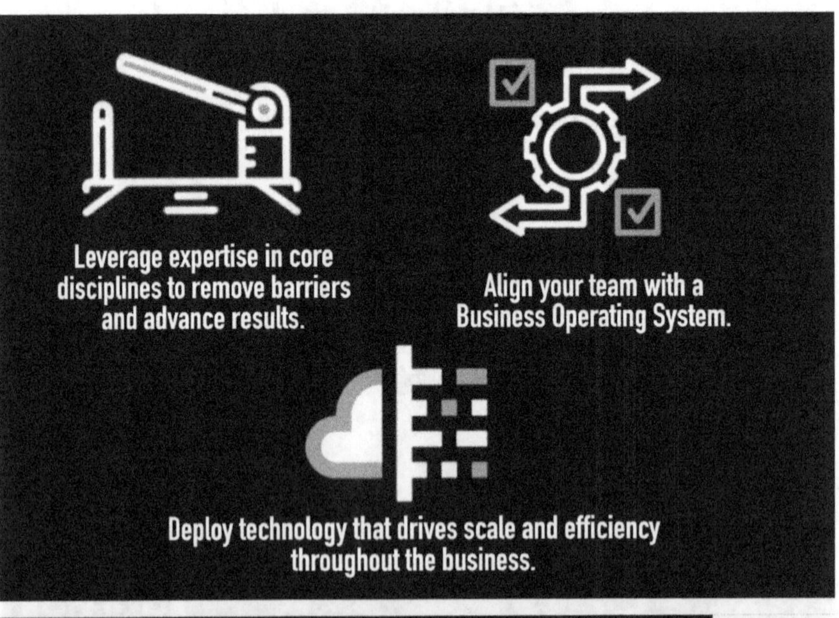

ImpactArchitects.io

EOS®
ENTREPRENEURIAL
OPERATING SYSTEM®
GET A GRIP ON YOUR BUSINESS
WITH THE ENTREPRENEURIAL OPERATING SYSTEM®
EOSWorldWide.com

THE TRACTION LIBRARY™

GETTING EVERYONE IN YOUR COMPANY ON THE SAME PAGE

TRACTION: *GET A GRIP ON YOUR BUSINESS*
Strengthen the Six Key Components® of your business using simple yet powerful tools and disciplines.

FOR EVERYONE

GET STARTED:

ROCKET FUEL: THE ONE ESSENTIAL COMBINATION
Dive into how the Visionary and Integrator duo can take their company to new heights.

FOR VISIONARIES & INTEGRATORS

GET A GRIP: AN ENTREPRENEURIAL FABLE
Follow this fable's characters as they learn how to run on EOS® and address real-world business situations.

FOR THE LEADERSHIP TEAM

WHAT THE HECK IS EOS?
Create ownership and buy-in from every employee in your organization, inspiring them to take an active role in achieving your company's vision.

FOR ALL EMPLOYEES, MANAGERS, & SUPERVISORS

HOW TO BE A GREAT BOSS!
Help bosses at all levels of your organization get the most from their people.

FOR LEADERS, MANAGERS, & SUPERVISORS

THE EOS LIFE
Learn how to create your ideal life by doing what you love, with people you love, making a huge difference, being compensated appropriately, and with time for other passions.

FOR ENTREPRENEURS & LEADERSHIP TEAMS

THE EOS MASTERY SERIES™
Dive deeper into each of the Six Key Components® for more masterful execution.

EOSWORLDWIDE.COM